RETIREMENT
THE
REVOLUTION

Spend More Worry Less™

RETIREMENT
THE
REVOLUTION

Spend More Worry Less™

DAVID KENNON

Library of Congress Cataloging-in-Publication Data
Kennon, David, 1976.

The Retirement Revolution: Spend More Worry Less.
By David Kennon. — Second Edition
Includes bibliographic notes and appendix.

ISBN: 978-0-692-19246-7
1. Retirement—Financial planning. 2. Retirement—Psychological aspects

Securities offered through First Allied Securities, Inc., A Registered Broker/Dealer Member: FINRA, SIPC. Advisory Services offered through First Allied Advisory Services, a Registered Investment Advisor. Kennon Financial & First Allied Securities/First Allied Advisory Services are not affiliated entities. The opinions expressed in this publication are those of the author and may not be the opinions of First Allied Securities, First Allied Advisory Services or their affiliates. The information has no regard to the specific investment objectives, financial situation, or particular needs of any specific recipient, and is intended for informational purposes only and does not constitute a recommendation, or an offer, to buy or to sell any securities or related financial instruments, nor is it intended to provide tax, legal or investment advice. We recommend that you procure financial and/or tax advice as to the implications (including tax) before implementing any strategy. There is no certainty that any strategy will be profitable or successful in obtaining your investment objectives.

Jacket design by Chris Alexander

Printed in the United States of America
by Serbin Print Marketing & Publishing, Sarasota, Florida

Thanks to my awesome wife, Dalanee,
and my just-as-awesome kids:
Jesse, Alex, Chris and Senay.
You are my greatest blessings.

CONTENTS

FOREWORD

Welcome to Sarasota, Florida. Home of sea breezes, jasmine blooms and all the good living you can handle. It's here in our little piece of paradise where I advise retirees and soon-to-be retirees on how to maximize their investments, with the goal of living the most financially empowered retirement they can imagine.

In addition to my investment advisory practice, I meet about 30 to 50 Baby Boomers each month through my Social Security education outreach classes.

Over the years, I've noted a startling pattern: practically no one, in my experience, is spending their retirement savings. All the while, their portfolio values keep mounting. This, to my mind, means no one is *living* their best retirement—at least, they are not living as free and fulfilling a retirement as they can afford.

What is going on? I hear so much fear and hesitation surrounding money from the Boomers I meet. It's my view that this trepidation is stopping an alarming number of retired Americans from fully enjoying their post-work life. They have saved so hard for years. And there is absolutely no need for the level of scrimping and making do that I see week after week.

I'll say it right now: The majority of Baby Boomers have way more money than they think. Or, more accurately, the money they *know* they have, will go further than they *think*. Most Baby

Boomers should feel empowered to start spending some of their savings on the *day* they retire. On the very first day.

The central point of this book is to say that you can spend more than you think, but that doesn't mean we are buying a reckless one-way ticket to Spendville, USA. We're spending smart, and yes, you'll be way more comfortable than you thought possible.

My approach is by no means outlandish: I am suggesting you spend five percent of your savings per year, one percentage point higher than the four percent conventional wisdom—an amount I believe to be unnecessarily conservative.

I believe you have an opportunity to make your retirement extraordinary. At the very least, you can banish your anxiety about your finances, and you can spend a little, to live a lot!

I call my approach the Retirement Revolution, because I'm literally asking retirees to turn on its head the traditional idea of retirement. I'm calling on you to think bigger, safe in the knowledge that you have the financial security to do so.

Before I go further, I want to share with you some assumptions that tie in with the premise of this book. You can spend some five percent of your retirement savings each year *if:*

- You have *at least* $200K in retirement savings.
- You have (or will have) a diversified portfolio of stocks and bonds with at least half of your investable funds in stocks.

If you are reading this book and you have less than $200K in investable assets, my message to you is not to spend as much as five percent of your savings each year. And, like everyone, you should consult directly with your financial advisor concerning your unique circumstances. Aside from my spending revolution message, the rest of my book applies to every Baby Boomer retiring today.

In Part One, I'll share the retirement myths many of us carry around with us, *and* why our retirements are much brighter than we think. In Part Two, we will get down to the nuts and bolts of revolutionizing your retirement by positioning yourself to be able to spend. In Part Three, we are going deeper into the revolution by exploring how the concept of retirement itself needs a rework. Baby Boomers have redefined expectations and ways of approaching life at every new stage they encounter, so why would retirement be any different?

You can spend more in your retirement and go live all the dreams you put on the shelf. Go forth into retirement bliss: take the cruise, buy the kitchen, join the circus and do any other thing, big or small, that your heart desires.

Well, OK, it's not quite that simple. We are going to dig deeper because there is a whole lot to talk about. Join me on this journey to reworking, revitalizing and reimagining your retirement. You've got a lot to plan, and a lot to look forward to. Let's get to work.

Here's to your best possible retirement!

Dave

INTRODUCTION

I'm going to share with you two hypothetical families, each with their own retirement scenarios. Their stories represent an amalgamation of common situations I have observed over the past 17+ years. I condense these stories together to help clarify my points.

The Smiths, and the Joneses, depict the challenges Baby Boomers face as they retire. The Smiths followed the traditional path of retirement. The Joneses took a lesser known path; a path I consider to be the empowered and informed option.

Introducing Mr. and Mrs. Smith

Mr. and Mrs. Smith were our picture-perfect couple. Jim Smith, 63, worked for a large telephone company for almost his entire adult life, working his way up to a middle-management position. Bev Smith taught third grade for nearly 40 years. She loved her students, and had no interest in becoming principal. Bev loved the kids, and the work of being a teacher.

Before retiring, Jim and Bev both felt a combination of relief and trepidation. Retirement was like a finish line to Jim, a line he looked forward to crossing, right up until he was about to cross it. Bev was driven by her work, but was ready to step off the pedal of the job's routine. As retirement was becoming more of a reality, their anxieties were mounting. The source of their concern? Money. They were concerned that would not have enough money to finance their whole retirements.

Rewind back to Bev and Jim's childhood. Our characters' *parents* came of age during the Depression, listening to penny-wise and pound-foolish proverbs. They had a radio positioned, center stage, in the living room where the family gathered and they listened to *The Shadow*, to Jack Benny, and from March 1933 to June 1944 to President Franklin Roosevelt's radio broadcasts, known as Fireside Chats. Most people who experienced the Depression lived the rest of their lives with more than a lingering suspicion about the stability of the economy. They watched every penny they spent and denied themselves most "wasteful" pleasures—which meant most pleasures, period.

Our Boomers were born into a time of relative new, post-Depression wealth. Their parents, while careful not to spend on frivolous things, were able to buy a family car, and a TV. Still, on a day-to-day basis, even with the occasional relative luxury, Jim and Bev were raised with the basic assumption that you saved hard, because you could never count on tomorrow's earnings.

The Smiths' views about retirement might have been shaped more by their upbringings than they would have liked to admit. Sure, Jim and Bev enjoyed a "wild youth," but that quickly passed, and they settled into the kind of life most Boomers did: working to get ahead, raising a family and going to Little League games and PTA meetings. They saved for the down payment on their home. They saved to pay for their three sons' college educations. And through it all, they managed to put a little away for their retirement.

They didn't scrimp. There were summer camps and sports leagues for the kids, as well as tutors if they fell behind in a subject. They lived a good life, but they were careful with their finances, saving more than they spent. Even though they never earned extraordinary salaries, Jim and Bev worked hard for their entire lives and carefully followed a prudent financial plan. Perhaps they didn't stick to a budget as ardently as their parents did, but they certainly saved diligently.

A home mortgage was the only debt the Smiths felt comfortable with, and they resisted buying anything that they couldn't pay for with cash. Credit cards, with their high interest rates, were a convenience they were not willing to risk; and if they did use them, they paid any balance within a month or two.

Jim and Bev were assiduous retirement savers. For almost their entire working lives, they saved 10 percent of their earnings, which they put directly into their 401(k)s and IRAs. The Smiths had the right attitude and good sense, and I doubt I could have plotted out a better financial path were I to have met with them 40 years ago.

Careful saving accumulated about $500,000 in retirement accounts. In addition, the Smiths had nearly $100,000 in the bank, spread between some CDs, savings and checking accounts.

Mr. and Mrs. Smith were typical Boomers: focused and industrious. They certainly were not entitled and selfish, as their generation is sometimes unfairly labelled. They worked hard, saved smartly, and were disciplined in their planning. Now, approaching retirement, they had questions about having enough money saved for their later years.

On the first day of their retirement, their pension and Social Security income looked as follows:

- Mrs. Smith was to receive a pension of $2,000 per month.
- Her Social Security check was to be about $1,500.
- Mr. Smith's Social Security check was to be about the same: $1,500.

The Smiths were debt-free and received about $5,000 a month—or, about $4,300 after taxes. Their expenses for a typical month were about $4,000. The Smith's finances looked pretty good. If they only relied on their retirement income, Jim and Bev would be accumulating $300 per month for discretionary spending. Not too shabby when you keep in mind they had some significant savings for unexpected expenses.

However, Mr. and Mrs. Smith were not pleased with this financial "outcome." Now on a fixed income, as they see it, $300 did not sound like a lot. Anything could upset the apple cart. They were already trying to think of ways to reduce their expenses, and certainly could not imagine tapping into any of those savings.

The reality was that Jim and Bev's hard work and savings put them in a very good position to enjoy their retirement. When I see Boomers with savings like Jim and Bev, I see a retirement of potential, fulfilled dreams and a meaningful post-work life.

But Jim and Bev were not reassured. To them, savings means "rainy-day" money. Untouchable money. That money wasn't there for them to spend; it was protection against unforeseeable events. Smart. We all need savings set aside for the "what ifs" that most of us will encounter. You know the kind of unplanned expenses I mean:

medical costs, dental work, a car, a new roof—big ticket items—all of which are taken into account during retirement planning.

Jim and Bev decided they would live on their existing budget of $5,000 a month and reduce their spending to make sure they had more "rainy day" funds set aside. Their savings were to remain untouched for those big expenses.

* * *

Imagine we are one year into the Smiths' retirement. True to their nature and habits, they were disciplined in that first year. After all, they are now living on a "fixed income." They did not go out to eat a lot but did occasionally visit a Denny's or a local Italian restaurant. And they always ordered the least expensive thing, and never anything from the bar. Wine and beer at restaurant prices? No way.

As for vacations, the Smiths enjoyed a few road trips to visit their kids' families and a couple weekend trips to nearby towns to go shopping for antiques. Just to look, not to buy, of course. The Smiths lived that first year of retirement with the conviction that they were on a fixed income, and would never again make money. Sure, they hadn't seen the grandkids as much as they had hoped. And it looked like that dream trip to New Zealand was never going to happen.

They did not want to end up like those retirees who they had been reading about, people who had to go back to work and take low-paying jobs just to make ends meet.

Does it sound like the Smiths are enjoying their retirement?

They might be enjoying the fact that they don't have to work, but the truth is they are economising to an unnecessary degree, second guessing so-called "lavish" decisions like dinners out, movies, plays and weekend vacations.

* * *

The years continued. All the while, the money they had worked so hard to save and invest into various financial vehicles grew. We can imagine the Smiths checking in on their monthly statements, fully aware that their nest egg had grown to be even bigger than when they started retirement. They were pleased when the funds rose, and overwhelmed with worry when they fell—which, of course, is why they wouldn't spend any of their savings. They thought the downswings of the market were more than enough risk to put on their savings. Adding the idea of spending any of those savings to their retirement equation, to them, was out of the question.

The numbers on the financial statements represented security to the Smiths. Jim and Bev have not allowed the money that those numbers represent to inform their sense of reality or to make any practical impact on their lives. Of course, they would have loved to have sent their grandson to the summer camp he kept talking about, and to have taken that dream trip around the world, but those kinds of big spends were just not prudent. The Smiths believed that their money could be gone in a flash, and that they needed to save every penny.

Imagine the years continued to pass. The statements arrived, month after month. Our annual account review meetings continued. With each passing year, the routines stayed the same and the Smiths got a little older. Their weekend vacations and car trips—their only travel "extravagance"—became less frequent. They continued to worry about that rainy day, and continued to stash away their savings.

"What if?" continued to define their retirement.

They believed they were, after all, on a fixed income.

Every year, I asked them the same question, "Are you enjoying your retirement?"

Every year, the answers were along of the lines of "Happy enough" and "Making do.

* * *

I picture Mr. and Mrs. Smith, in their mid-eighties, sitting at their kitchen table eating breakfast when the mail comes. Mr. Smith collects the mail and there, among catalogs, is their financial statement. Once again, they open it and pore over the numbers.

"Would you look at that!" Mr. Smith says with a sense of amazement. He then sighs.

Mrs. Smith leans closer.

They stare at the numbers. Over the course of their retirement, that $500,000 has inexplicably grown to $1 million. It happened so gradually that they had not really taken note of it.

Mr. Smith raises his eyes and looks at Mrs. Smith. "We're millionaires," he says, the phrase sounding unreal on his tongue.

How had that happened?

You may have thought they would be thrilled to realize they had a lot of money. More than they ever dreamed of. More than enough for a rainy day. More than enough to enjoy their retirement. There was only one problem. Now that they had the means to enjoy their retirement, they were unable to take advantage of it and were too old to want to.

For all their smart discipline and good planning, they had outsmarted themselves. They had been so prudent and so careful that they found themselves with more than they ever believed was possible, yet those funds would provide them virtually no benefit.

In my estimation, that is the very definition of irony.

I cannot be critical of Mr. and Mrs. Smith. Everything they did made perfect sense. Their hard work, their determined saving, their financial caution … it had all paid off. Hadn't it? Their home mortgage had been paid off long before. They had no debt. Their sons were doing well. They were retired.

But, the dreams they had were unfulfilled. The trip to New Zealand? It stayed on the dream shelf. No stories to share, memories to cherish or photographs to show to their grandchildren. Mrs. Smith had always dreamed of buying a pair of Merino wool mittens from a sheep farm near Auckland. Bev spent some of her days in retirement on arts and crafts and dearly wanted to visit the notable CraftWorld store, filled with native arts and crafts. They both wanted to take their grandchildren to Auckland's *Lord of the Rings* movie set, to see where the story was filmed. And they wanted to travel south over the Bombay Hills.

Now, when they think about their money, they contemplate how nice it will be to pass it along to their children. Generous, perhaps. But that isn't what they saved that money for. That money was supposed to be for their retirement.

Mr. and Mrs. Smith reach across their kitchen table and hold hands. They look into each other's eyes and both recognize the same emotion: regret.

There are no sadder words in the English language than "could have." They could have lived a fuller, more active retirement. They could have enjoyed their lives more. But they didn't.

Five years or so later, Mr. and Mrs. Smith passed away. Their account was valued at more than $1.2 million. Much of it, according to their wishes, was split evenly among their three sons. The middle son, always a bit more irresponsible than the other two, went through his inheritance quickly, annoying his brothers.

More troubling, there was one account that wasn't clearly dealt with in the will. The beneficiary designations were dated. The distribution was unequal among the three sons.

That prompted vague threats of legal action. Real acrimony arose. Relationships were strained. Marriages were affected. If Mr. and Mrs. Smith had known what was happening, they would have been, as the saying goes, "turning over in their graves."

The relationships between the sons continued to be strained to the point that they rarely spoke with one another except to argue about their parents' estate. They withheld invitations for birthdays, graduations and weddings because of unresolved quarrels.

Meanwhile, each of the sons dealt with his portion of the inheritance differently. One, as we know, went through it quickly. One, much like his parents, invested it and watched it begin to grow.

The third son used his inheritance to buy things he should never have purchased, such as a vacation home he didn't really need or particularly want. The vacation home became a financial burden when property values dropped. For Bev and Jim, leaving their retirement savings to their children just seemed like right thing to do.

And that is the legacy of Mr. and Mrs. Smith—wonderful, good, lovely people who sacrificed for the what ifs that never came.

* * *

Let's Meet Mr. and Mrs. Jones

Sandra and Bruce Jones were in a similar starting position to Bev and Jim Smith. Bruce was ready to retire after teaching high school for 40 years. Sandra was ready to leave her middle-management position at a bank. Approaching 65, they had about $500,000 in various retirement accounts.

At 65, they retired and began receiving Social Security and their pensions, which combined were just enough to cover their monthly expenses.

However, unlike Bev and Jim Smith, they had a different perspective on how to manage their money. That money they had saved for retirement? They intended to use it.

Mr. Jones joked, "I will consider myself a success if the last check I ever write bounces."

The Joneses wanted an advisor who would show them how to put their savings to work so they would never run out of money in retirement. They were open to seeing how they could afford to spend some of their money.

Just as they had worked and planned to manage their savings leading up to their retirement, they would now have to do the same in retirement.

The Jones were interested in leaving funds to their kids, if there were any left over. But first, they would take care of their own needs in retirement. They had worked hard to make sure they had positioned themselves well. They had financed their children's college, and even with the down payments on their homes. They'd even loan money to their children, should the need arise.

Mr. and Mrs. Jones believed they had saved money for a reason. And that reason was to spend it on living. From the beginning of their retirement planning, upon their first contribution to an IRA, they agreed that the money would be for them.

"We traveled a little," Mr. Jones said. "Trips with the kids. Washington D.C., Cooperstown. Now, we want to travel for us."

They agreed that they had saved money for the purpose of enjoying themselves in retirement. Their goal from the very beginning had been to responsibly and mindfully spend their money so that they could enjoy their retirement and have nothing left over when they die.

Given their ages and the health of their investments, they were able to reasonably take $2,000 per month from their retirement portfolio. That extra money meant the difference between just getting by and living an inspired retirement. At a five percent withdrawal rate, Sandra and Bruce's portfolio would not be in any real danger of disappearing. The goal was to continue to earn interest and dividends which approximated that withdrawal.

So the Joneses, right from the get-go of their retirement, made it their mission to live the rest of their lives as fully and richly as they could. The extra money allowed them to feel generous. They helped pay for a grandchild's piano lessons. They took their children and grandchildren on a week-long vacation once per year.

They found great satisfaction in giving money to their church and helping to support its scholarship fund.

When Mr. Jones' sister became a widow and faced unexpected expenses, they were able to help her. They put money into their grandchildren's college accounts. They were thrilled to discover how enjoyable and meaningful they found the act of giving.

Mr. Jones volunteered his time by going to the high school to tutor students who needed additional help with their studies. He lectured at the local library on topics he taught in the high school.

Mr. and Mrs. Jones also found that they enjoyed just having fun and spoiling themselves in ways they had never before thought possible. They experienced some luxurious treats like day spas, desserts and trips overseas, and they also took care of themselves with private yoga classes and working with a nutritionist.

I press fast forward and envision them 20 years into their retirement, sitting at their kitchen table when the mail arrives. Along with the junk mail, they find their quarterly financial statement. Opening the envelope and reading the document, Mr. Jones nods his head in amazement. He hands the document to his wife.

"Would you look at that," he says, pointing at the statement's numbers and grinning.

She perches her glasses on her nose and peers closely at the figures. "My, my," she says and then sighs.

On the statement is their balance: $500,000. Exactly the amount with which they had started their retirement 20 years before. All of the things they had done and enjoyed over the past 20 years had not diminished that amount by one cent. All the money they had spent was simply refilled by the modest returns on their portfolio. Oh, they are not millionaires by any stretch. Their retirement account hasn't grown to $2 million or $3 million. Their children will not receive windfall inheritances when they are gone. But they have lived a wonderful 20 years of a fulfilling retirement. They did not withdraw from life to worry about the "what ifs" of their finances. Instead, they planned for life and engaged with it. Their children and grandchildren received the best of that money because they were able to share it with them for all of these years.

They supported the things they believed in. They helped those they loved. And they enjoyed one another.

Smart financial planning, in my opinion, allowed all of that to happen for the Joneses. Their generous perspective and intelligent decision-making also contributed. They went into retirement with informed optimism, knowing that they had an investment plan that allowed them to spend more than most allow themselves to. They started retirement with the same amount of money as the Smiths, but rather than having a million in the bank, they had priceless memories for themselves, and even some for their kids.

"How rich," said Mrs. Jones. Looking at each other across their kitchen table, the Joneses smiled and nodded their heads in agreement. "Blessed" is another word that comes to mind.

When they passed five years later, $500,000 was split evenly between their children. It was more money than they had wanted or expected to inherit. They had learned from their parents that the real joy of money is in how you use it to live a generous and meaningful life.

At their funerals, everyone had a story to tell about Mr. and Mrs. Smith: the time they'd vacationed together, and the time when Grandma and Grandpa came to a piano recital that couldn't have happened without their generosity.

Think of how Mr. and Mrs. Smith lived in retirement. Now think of Mr. and Mrs. Jones and what their retirement looked like.

Which retirement do you want?

PART ONE

CHAPTER ONE:

Spendophobia: It's Time To Break The Pandemic
Get your facts first, then you can distort them as you please.
Mark Twain

When I first sit down with a prospective client, I ask straightforward questions about their finances. Almost everyone I see has some savings: some money in a 401(k) plan, IRA, Roth IRA or annuity. And everyone, of course, has social security. Most of them have additional non-retirement savings such as CDs, savings accounts and money markets. Once I review sources of income, assets and savings, my next question is usually one they don't expect.

I ask: "So when do you plan to start *spending* that money?"
The typical answer: "When I need to."

When I *need* to. Think about that for a second. Folks have toiled and saved their whole lives only to have money for when they need it—and that is a very difficult point in time to define. Virtually never do I meet a person who has a plan for how they will spend some of their funds as part of an intentional, fulfilling post-work life.

A number of my clients who attended my social security classes—those who had looked into the issue before I asked or had spoken to one or more financial advisors—venture a more specific answer: "When I'm 70 and a half." They know that they'll be penalized if they don't cash out based on the "required minimum distributions" rules set by the government. (Sidenote: 70 and a half is not the correct answer, and I'll explain more about social security strategy in Part Two—stayed tuned.)

When I speak to people in their 80s and 90s, the impact of the "only spend when you need to" mentality really hits home. I ask my "Silent Generation" and "Greatest Generation" clients what advice they would give newbie retirees. The same variation of a theme crops up time and time again. And I wish we could put their message on every TV show, infomercial and billboard. Their message is so important that I'm going to set it apart from the rest of the page below. May it imprint on every fiber of your being before we go further on this journey.

The Great and Silent Generation generally wish they had:

- Spent their money to bring more joy, satisfaction and happiness.
- Planned better, done more and worried less.
- Been empowered to spend more on their dreams.

They certainly could have been empowered to live their dreams and sought joy with the financial plans they had put in place. Yet today, they sit with cash in the bank, more than they know what to do with.

Too many people have found themselves in the "enviable" position of leaving behind a healthy savings account. Why? Because they deferred enjoyment. Because "when I need to" never came. They lived their retirement frugally, pinching pennies. They lived on their Social Security and possibly a work pension. They didn't spend a penny of their investment savings, which continued to grow while they squirrelled all that live-your-life money away.

For what? And for whom? Sure, if they absolutely needed a bit of money, they took it out of savings, but only the absolute minimum needed. Meanwhile, the funds racked up while would-be memories were left on the shelf, a joyful retirement unrealized.

I hear the same two phrases over and over again:

"You never know" and "What *if?*"

You never do know. Something could always go wrong.

Because, conventional wisdom often states, if something happens, you want your money there when you need it. When these retirees reached their 80s and 90s, they discovered that the "what if's" never happened, and now they have more money than they would ever be able to spend. Their investments had continued to grow over time, as did their savings. They had the means to really enjoy their lives … but neither the time nor the energy.

Scarcity Mentality in Boomers: The Hangover of the Great Depression

Meet Ted and Alice. They represent to me a "typical" Baby Boomer couple—if there really is such a thing. Their story is a composite of stories I have heard from couples over time.

Fresh on the retirement road, Ted and Alice had worked and saved prudently throughout their adult lives. They shared a palpable mistrust for the reliable flow of money, so they stocked away their funds with care. They learned this "mind the pennies" approach from their parents.

Their parents kept cash, bills, and change in labeled jars: one marked "Groceries," another marked 'Electric' and so on. A prudent way to budget money, which many people still do today, often with envelopes or, more so, budgeting software.

Their parents never took from one jar to cover an expense from another jar. If they took from the electric jar, there might not be enough to cover the electric bill. Same with rent. Their parents always paid bills in full, and on time. Nothing wrong with that. The idea of credit was unheard of. The only debt they would know was to buy a house. They owned a single, used car, paid for in full and in cash.

I completely respect those who use credit sparingly, keep debt in check, and are willing to defer gratification until they have the money. This very mentality passed down from parents is a big reason why so many soon-to-be-retirees I see are now in such good shape financially. But, when taken too far, the results are heartbreaking.

Alice's mom and dad paid for their car and house many years before they retired, and were glad simply to live in their home without a mortgage.

Of course, they kept their money held safely in the bank in a specified amount. Never more than the $100,000 that FDIC insurance would cover. Instead they placed the accounts in separate financial institutions to comply with those guidelines. They received a little interest from their CDs and savings. As long as they didn't lose anything, their financial lives were in order.

Once Alice's parents retired, they didn't really do much of anything. No trips or particular hobbies. No volunteering. They were content to mull around, and not to spend any money.

Like many Boomers, Ted and Alice want something different from their retirement. Their kids all live across the country. Just visiting them would keep them busy. Still, Ted and Alice want to do a lot more traveling, outside of visiting their kids and their families.

Ted dreams of playing a number of the world's incredible golf courses—to follow the trail of Jack Nicklaus when he won the British Open, for example. They'd go Scotland's Muirfield Village Golf Club, and from there on to London, where Alice would love to visit Harrods and visit the historical sites and art museums.

Ted and Alice, in short, want to live a happy, active and inspired life full of travel and experience—a much more expansive view of retirement than their parents.

But they both agreed that they had been infected by some of their parents' attitudes about money and investing. Alice's parents would make a face every time they took the family on an "extravagant" vacation. That trip to the Grand Canyon, when the kids were 7 and 5, was viewed as pretty over the top.

Ted and Alice's kids had drama and music lessons. They played little league baseball. The family took trips together. Ted and Alice did not think twice about using credit to buy cars, vacations, and even a timeshare. Alice had more jewelry than her mother ever imagined having. Their friends spent quite a bit more than them, but relative to their parents, Ted and Alice already lived large.

Still, Ted and Alice discovered that, as they got older, they were becoming more and more like their parents. Alice would start to sound like her mother with the classic dinner table admonishment, "Finish your dinner. Children are starving all around the world."

Ted heard his dad's frugal approach to spending at the checkout more and more as he neared retirement.

Even having purchased the nice home, cars and life experiences their parents considered extravagant, they saved diligently for their retirement. Sure, they could have saved more; their retirement was not "as much as it could have been."

Now, as they considered how they would live their retirement, they found themselves unsettled by what was ahead, often in ways and with emotions that they were not used to dealing with. Now that they would no longer be earning, shouldn't they stop spending? What kind of picture does not earning, and therefore spending, mean for their dreams?

It's one thing to save and invest while you're working and making a decent income. But when the time comes to stop working, and the paychecks stop rolling in, I have found that the thinking changes radically.

I've heard the Teds and Alices of this world start saying things like: "This is it. I don't have another chance at securing my future. If I lose my money, there is no way for me to make more and refill my account. I'll end up flipping burgers at 85."

With no other options in their minds, they fall back on the default setting any human being would have with this fearful mindset. It is this fear that could derail the joy you deserve in retirement.

Baby Boomers grew up in the shadows of the "Greatest Generation," hearing horror stories of the Great Depression. Your generation came of age with that fear of winding up penniless, and have been sold to, based on that fear, by advisors, the media and anyone else who makes money from your investments. We've learned that we have to hold onto our money so that we are prepared for recessions, and, heaven forbid, the Great Depression 2.0.

The Baby Boomer generation spans some two decades, born between 1946 and 1965. It's worth noting that Baby Boomers are a diverse bunch—age-wise and socio-economically. (And as I said in the foreword, this book really applies to those *with* at least $200K in retirement savings.) A range of 20 years means that we have folks just about to retire and folks who have been retired for 10 years or so—it pays well to listen to the preceding generations. Your peers are possibly just retired and going into the freedom years, as I like to call them. And, as a group, you have more money than any other generation. Depending on reports, your generation currently holds between 50 and 80 percent of the nation's personal net worth.[1]

You've encountered a few recessions and financial setbacks. Boomers experienced a stock market calamity in the 1980s—including the October 1987 mini-crash (from computerized large-volume trades by institutional investors), then the "Dot-Com" bubble in the late 1990s, the terrorist attacks in 2001, and the Great Recession from December 2007 to June 2009.

You may have college-aged children and grandchildren to provide for (some 18 percent of Boomers help support their kids, and 9 percent help support their grandkids[2]). As a generation, you have worked hard, saved, and been one of the most charitable, giving, and community-oriented age collectives seen to date. Recall President John Kennedy's 1961 "Ask not …" speech, and President Ronald Reagan's 1987 speech, "Tear down this wall …" — both speeches rallied Boomers to be one of the most engaged generations in history.

You know that your generation will live longer than your parents' generation. You also likely know that you live larger than your parents' generation, and have greater expectations from your retirement than your parents. You hear about rising healthcare costs and how Medicare will not meet those costs, and then what about longer-term living and care plans down the road?

All of this information wraps up in a big ol' box of financial anxiety:

Recessions

+ responsibilities

+ uncertain healthcare costs

+ Depression era mentality

=

Feeling unprepared for retirement.

That's a lot of concern to go around one person's head. And you are smart to address your financial reality. The fact is that when you make a post-retirement financial plan, you take into account unexpected costs, and the cost of healthcare. Preparedness is smart. You're aware, prudent and thoughtful ... and a little caution has likely served you well in life. The problem is that, and historical stock returns support my thinking here, the lack of spending I see among my client groups is *over*cautious.

"Overcaution" costs you more in lost experience
than it protects you against life's inevitable expenses.

The reality for many retirees who have retirement savings is that they end up with more money in their 80s and 90s than they started with in their 60s.

Retirement expert Andrew Biggs recently cited data from the Federal Reserve Consumer Survey, to highlight how average retirement savings fare across three decades. Many retirees are not touching their retirement savings, leaving behind significantly more than when they started retirement. According to the data, retirees aged 65 to 67 in the year 1989 showed a median household net work of $122,318 in 2013 dollars. By the ages of 89 to 91, the same group had a median amount of $202,400.[3]

Take a minute to think about just how much *more* money they ended up with: *around 60 percent*! In my opinion, these retirees found themselves richer because their invested savings continued to appreciate faster than they spent their money. But for what good? It turns out retirement had not been nearly as expensive as they thought. Imagine what they could have done with the money, safe in the knowledge that they had a solid financial plan in place. At what cost did these retirees have larger numbers in their bank account? What did each higher number represent? A lot of missed life experience. A ton of unrealized dreams. Decades of not participating in travel, charity, education, family—or whatever means the most to them. Great, you've got an extra $80,000 in the bank, but is the extra cash worth if it goes untouched? Imagine you are one of the people who ends up 60 percent richer at age 90. Will you be as fit and able to realize the dreams you have now? Those extra tens of thousands of dollars could well be your payment for sacrificing an extraordinary retirement—whatever extraordinary looks like to you.

We hear in the media that we don't have enough saved for retirement. It might be true for those without retirement savings. What isn't true is that those of us *with* retirement savings should live in fear that we don't have enough saved. Researchers at Texas Tech University found that retirees, as a whole, are not spending as much as they could be.[4] (And they cited numerous studies that showed that retirees usually pass away with more money than they had on the day they retired.) The researchers sought to find out if retirees are spending an amount that would put them in danger of running out of money. They wanted to know the impact of our living longer and the possibility of low asset returns. They reviewed the financial data of 835 retirees, and organized them into five quintiles of wealth.

Using data from the longitudinal Health and Retirement Study (HRS)[5] they found that all five groups' financial assets increased between 2000 and 2010 (which was a historically terrible decade in the stock market). The researchers found that retirees in the top three quintiles consumed much less than they had available to spend—they did not manage to spend their monthly income, let alone tap into their savings.

Thank you, academics, for showing what I've long observed in my practice: your money goes further in retirement than you think. I've seen so many retired people too scared to spend any of their savings, and invariably the same thing happens: they reach their 80s and 90s with *significantly* more money in the bank than when they started retirement.

In my opinion, spending five percent of your income is a sustainable withdrawal rate—assuming you have at least $200K in investable assets. Allowing yourself to spend, according to a solid plan, means YOU get to put your money to work as you see fit.

The fear around spending in retirement is so prevalent, we have a term for it. I hear the word *"spendophobia"* more and more in general parlance.

Financial therapy really *is* a thing now. Scholars at a nonprofit group, Financial Therapy Association, study and counsel individuals about the challenges they face with money and the behavioral, psychological, relational and emotional hurdles they have when it comes to money. Financial therapists are cropping up all over the country as the need clearly grows.

I'm glad that financial therapy is growing as a discipline. I hear so much regret from members of Silent Generation, and in turn, so much fear from Baby Boomers. Over time, it just kills me inside. The pain of downright lack of living is unnecessary, and that's the most frustrating part. Folks are not spending nearly as much as they could be, because they *feel* that they do not have enough money saved for retirement. Nearly always, they *do* have enough money saved.

Not only do they have enough money saved for retirement—they have enough money to spend in retirement.

You are in better shape than you think. I have a feeling you've not been told before that you can spend on day one of your retirement. When we talk about retirement, we usually talk about cutting back, living on less. We talk about Social Security falling apart, and the retirement crisis that affects the whole nation.

Let's confront that elephant in the room next.

CHAPTER TWO:

The Retirement Crisis That Isn't... Not For You

Today more people believe in UFOs than believe that
Social Security will take care of their retirement.
Scott Cook

Eighty-eight percent of Americans believe that the nation faces a retirement crisis.[6] That figure is consistent across all gender, income, ages and political party affiliations. The media is packed with stories of America's retirement crisis: stories of Baby Boomers living longer than any generation before, Social Security running out, and how the average Baby Boomer has not saved enough for the long retirement they will likely have.

There's the problem with that logic: folks have more savings than gets reported. The Census Bureau's data concerning retirement income does not take into account income derived from cashing out IRAs and 401(K)s; it only takes into account income that is paid out regularly. The 10th percentile of 65-69 year olds have an average of around $141K in net worth, and the 90th percentile has approximately $2M.[7] This figure accounts for more than IRAs and

401(K)s; home value, for example, but you get the point: we read all kinds of stats about the financial health of your fellow Boomers, but you are not being given *all* the information.

I fully admit that the people I work with have more money than other segments of the population. Boomers who don't have any savings may not be living extravagant retirements, but they are not penniless, thanks to a still solvent Social Security (we'll get to why Social Security isn't going broke shortly).

So what do the bank accounts of Americans in their 80s look like? In other words, after 20 years of retirement, do we have anything left in the bank? The Employee Benefit Research Institute found 20.6 percent of those who die above the age of 85 have no assets, other than housing, and 12 percent have no assets whatsoever, counting only on social security. Think about that: only 12 percent … that's a pretty positive number overall. I don't mean to sound glib, but when we reframe the number, things look pretty good for America's current retirees—88 percent of which have a home and money in the bank to retire with, and 79.4 percent with savings, retirement plans and assets of varying amounts.[8] And let's remember, we have social security income as a safety net.

It *is* fair to say that we do potentially have a *future* retirement crisis. Millenials are saving more than Gen X, but only two-thirds of the population has access to an employer-sponsored retirement plan.[9] One in three Americans do not have retirement savings.

Those who do not have savings and assets do not fit into the five percent spend plan I'm suggesting to you. But this is not *your* situation. When we hear the media talking about the Retirement Crisis, we will do well to keep in mind that …

- The "retirement crisis" does not apply to the Baby Boomer generation as a whole.
- Dialogue surrounding a retirement crisis usually includes all generations, not just Baby Boomers (younger generations have not saved as much as your group).
- Baby Boomers who do not have assets do still have the safety net of Social Security (it is *not* defunct).

A far bigger crisis, to me, is that people in their 80s and 90s have sacrificed unnecessarily during their retirement. They could have afforded to spend more. Even after having spent some of their savings, many people in this age group would have more money in their savings accounts than when they started retirement.

So why does this spendophobia happen? Why do smart people not spend their money, when, with a solid investment plan in place, they could be living a little larger on five percent of their pie each year?

Five Retirement Myths Busted!

We all have beliefs and assumptions surrounding money that frankly would not hold up were we to try them in court. We build up these beliefs through our experiences, watching our parents' retirements, and taking in stories from the media.

Most all of the information we hear about retirement is generalized, if not sensationalized. I want to take a minute to say that our beliefs about money are commonly shared. We are not stupid for having self-limiting beliefs about our finances. By our nature, we pay attention to dramatic news.

As a result of absorbing catastrophic thinking from the news, many of us hold onto beliefs about retirement that aren't so. If you buy in to any of these five myths, I want to you to banish them to a dusty abyss because they're holding you back and literally robbing you of the retirement you deserve.

Let's go ahead and slay retirement-limiting myths that have no place in the empowered Baby Boomer's mind. Ready? Let's do this.

Myth 1: *"I need to have $1 million to retire."*

Reality: *There is no standard amount of money that you need to retire.*

It all depends on your savings, your monthly budget and your expectations. Someone with $200,000 in savings and a budget of $3,000 a month is probably going to be just fine. Someone with $2 million in savings and a budget of $40,000 a month is probably in trouble.

The average retired American, aged 65-74, spends around $48,885 a year (a little over $4,000 a month).[10] The average monthly spend decreases for those older than 75 to $36,673 annually (just over $3,000 a month). When invested in the stock market, $200,000 can provide the dividends and growth required to live during retirement. A million bucks isn't necessarily the amount required to live a good retirement.

I cannot wait for you to do my retirement budget exercise in Chapter 8, because you may see *just how well prepared you are* for retirement once you do. But first, let's knock this myth at its source: the stories we tell ourselves and each other.

According to the Insured Retirement Institute, just 23 percent of Boomers believe they will have enough money to last throughout retirement.[11] The same study of Boomer Expectations found that a third of those with retirement savings have saved upwards of $250,000.

Women of the Boomer generation are unfortunately more likely to feel, and in reality *be* less well prepared for, retirement than men. Longer life expectancies, a greater likelihood of taking on caregiver roles and working part-time, and the gender pay gap means the average Boomer woman has less in retirement savings than her male counterpart. The National Retirement Institute found that women over 65 currently receive about 33 percent less than men in retirement income. Women are also 80 percent more likely to live in poverty during retirement than men.[12]

All that said, if you are reading this book, and you have $200,000 saved in your retirement account, these stats do not reflect your reality. I hear a lot of anxiety from female and male Boomers alike. It's natural to feel anxious when our society operates on the idea that you need a million bucks in the bank to retire. It's a huge number that is out of reach for many hard-working Americans. It's also not necessary. You can have a great retirement on a whole lot less than a cool million.

If you have retirement savings of $100K you are going to be OK ... you have Social Security to back you up. If you have $200K, you are set. I'm going to show you why when we slay Myth #2.

Myth 2: *Income stops or reduces significantly when you get your final paycheck.*

Reality: *A retirement plan that provides monthly income can more than meet your budget needs.*

Retirement does not mean you stop creating income. Your portfolio keeps working for you once you retire. The one variable that is invariably missed by many retirees is that their money *will keep working for them once they stop working*. You can't just look at your nest egg and divide it by the number of years that you may live. You're missing the most powerful point. A diversified portfolio of stocks and bonds between now and the end of your life should return, in my opinion, at least an average annual return of 5 percent per year. If it doesn't, it is the first time in modern economic history where it hasn't.[13] People typically see an increase in assets over time during retirement— with more money at the end of their retirement than they had at the beginning.[14]

When you combine your pension plan income with your strategically timed social security income, you might be pleasantly surprised at your monthly income. *Then* add your 5 percent spending slice from your invested assets each year (divided across 12 months)—you will be surprised at just how much income you have.

Correctly set up, your portfolio could provide plenty of income for emergencies *and* fun.

Myth 3: *You need about 80 percent of your final income to live in retirement.*

Reality: *If you do need that amount, it's hopefully because you are having an awesome retirement!*

You most likely have fewer expenses in retirement than during your working life. A common rule of thumb is that retirees need about 80 percent of their pre-retirement income to maintain their lifestyle after leaving the workforce. They call this amount the "replacement rate." I believe this amount is overkill, but we work with it in the name of prudence.

While healthcare expenses may go up (not necessarily right away, but years down the road), you may well spend less on day-to-day living, because you have more time. You'll keep some financial consistencies—insurance payments, utilities and the like— but you also may spend less on the conveniences full-time workers spend their money on out of necessity. The Government Accountability Office found that people in early retirement (65-69) spent 23 percent less than during their pre-retirement days— transportation, clothing and food spending were the main areas of spend reduction. The difference in spending is even more shocking if you compare spending rates of people in their late 40s to early 70s—a whopping 41 percent.[15]

You're more likely to have lower household expenses, as your mortgage may be paid off. (Though you can still retire and spend if you do have a mortgage—assuming you have a solid plan.) Once you've evaluated how much you need to live each month, you can help ensure your investment income meets that amount.

You receive a set amount from your pension plan, and your social security. While your investment account can fluctuate in terms of returns, you can have solid income streams from those accounts and, planned appropriately, you can take out a consistent amount even in down markets. Measure those incomes against your debts and expenses—and your projected expenses over the many different stages of your retirement, and you are prepared. I can hear you calling out the insecurity of the stock market and the insolvency of Social Security ... which is why I will take down these next two myths next.

Myth 4: *The stock market is too volatile for post-retirement investing.*

Reality: *Over time, the market has returned an annualized rate of over eight percent.*

Imagine you started retirement in 1997 with $100K. You invested your $100K in the S&P Index (the largest 500 stocks in the U.S. market). You took out five percent of your $100K ($5K) per year for 20 years. How much was your investment worth in 2017?

Based on the historical averages, the answer is a cool $145K, and some change. (Remembering that past performance is never a guarantee of future results.) You ended up with $45K more than your initial investment, even after withdrawing $5,000 (five percent of your original savings), each year for 20 years. Had you invested $100K the year prior, the results would have been even more pronounced, with an estimated 2016 balance of nearly $215K. Frankly, there are much more lucrative 20-year periods, for example: 1981 to 2001 with $100K turning to $1.2M, but this level of return is more of an outlier.

Look in the Appendix for my Rolling Periods report which shows you S&P returns over 20-year periods from 1931 to 2017. The historical returns you see in the table radically altered my own investing philosophy. The data is very eye-opening. Each line of information gives you a sense of what would have happened had you retired and invested your money in the stock market at any point in modern economic history—*while* you were withdrawing five percent of your account balance each year.

39

So how and why did this happen?

The S&P returned an average of 7.19 percent per year from 1997 to 2017, while you were disbursing your five percent spending money each year. Mostly you did not even touch the principal, because your returns were mostly above five percent. You reinvested any dividends not paid out as income, so, on average, you reinvested 2.19 percent each year into your original investment principal.

1997-2017 was a tough 20 years: the Great Recession happened during that time. Remember the biggest market price drop since the Great Depression? Yep, that happened in 2008.

Many of us feel that the stock market is unpredictable and dangerous. Despite what people are led to believe about the stock market, it has a remarkably consistent (and successful) track record—over time.

More on this in Chapter 7, when I dive deeper into the movements of the stock market, and some tips on rising above stock market drama with some serious historical perspective.

Myth 5: *Social Security is going broke.*

Reality: *Social Security is not going broke any time soon, not for you.*

I stay current with developments within the Social Security Administration, and I see no evidence that elected officials will agree that your benefits are going to be eliminated. Is the topic a political football? Often, it is. Luckily for you, it is easier for politicians to kick that can down the road. Your kids' kids may need to worry a bit, but you do not.

In its 82-year history, Social Security has collected just shy of $20 trillion and paid out just over $17 trillion. That leaves $2.8 trillion at the end of 2016. Social Security and Medicare expenses will grow in excess of the GDP growth through to the mid- 2030s. Baby Boomers are retiring, and the supporting workforce is smaller than the number of Boomers, thanks to lower birth rates. Good news for world population levels; bad news for Social Security. This doesn't impact you, though you'll likely hear otherwise.

Gen Z may well pay the price, as will the next generation after them. But your generation is pretty sorted in terms of social security. Social Security is 75 percent funded through 2091. That's a lot better than most people know.

According to House Majority Leader Eric Cantor, *"The starting point in any plan has got to be that we need to distinguish between those at or nearing retirement. Anyone 55 or older in this country has got to know that their Social Security benefits will not be changed."*

A couple of simple fixes can restore social security:

a) Increase payroll taxes by 2 percent.
b) Increase the earnings cut-off for payroll taxes.

Again, not your problem, but politicians on both sides of the aisle will have to come together to sort out Social Security. And as as I said earlier, we are going to talk Social Security strategy in Part Two, so hang tight, friends. A little smart planning and you will be getting the most out of your social security.

Myth 6: *"I need to stay on top of my portfolio daily."*

Reality: *Only do this if you want to go crazy for no good reason.*

People have a tendency to think, "I need to continually adjust my investments, watch financial news shows, and check my phone 10 times a day to see what the Dow Jones is doing," in order to have a successful portfolio. No, you don't.

During the 1970s and '80s, people who invested received market news once a week (gasp!). Years before that, ticker tapes were in fashion, and only the very wealthy had them. Although today we have the Internet to broadcast financial events constantly, there's no need to waste your energy watching every change.

Even those proclaimed financial "experts" who *do* sleep with one eye on the stock market channel don't have a grand secret to making money off the market. There's no magic tricks to pull, nor a secret map to follow leading to a treasure trove of stock market profits.

You can lay back, relax and get off your phone or computer. The Dow Jones isn't going to pull a fast one on you any time soon.

Have faith in the long-term value of your investment portfolio. Look at returns over a 20-year period since the Great Depression, and you'll see a consistent upward trajectory over time. There are scaremongers and well-intentioned market experts who don't think this pattern will continue into the future, but I believe they are underestimating the consistent drive of humans to create wealth and deliver value through the markets. The contents of your investment portfolios may change—for example, your investments may become more global over time as wealth increases around the world, but I believe we have every reason to, on balance, be optimistic about the future of the markets.

Myth 7: *"I need to have my house paid off before I retire."*

Reality: *It feels good to be debt-free but it is not a prerequisite for retiring.*

As long as your retirement budget can handle the payment, you can retire confidently with a mortgage. Lots of people have a mortgage in retirement. According to Money-Zine™, more than half of people over 65 still have mortgages. Twenty- three percent of those people are over 75.[16]

A lot of people think about cashing in their IRAs and 401k accounts to pay off their mortgages. In the VAST majority of cases, this is a big NO!

Cashing out your pre-tax retirement savings triggers taxation. Significant taxation. I've seen many folks who had cashed out tens of thousands of dollars to pay off their mortgage. I've literally seen people cash out $100,000—in ONE chunk—which means they have taken in $100,000 in *income* and triggered a higher tax bracket than they would have had otherwise. You could end up paying between 20-40 percent in tax to cash out $100,000. That's a lot of wasted money. Your retirement accounts are designed for you to take out regular income, to live on, month to month. You still pay tax, but it's in digestible amounts, over time—in a reasonable tax bracket.

Let's also remember you would potentially lose returns from your invested assets if you were to cash out your retirement accounts. That's a lot of unnecessary loss. A better plan is to take out a little bit of money from your IRA or 401K *over time*. You can pay down your mortgage faster than your loan repayment schedule, without paying unnecessary taxes and missing out on potential returns. Hey, you can even you use your five percent spend money if paying your mortgage down is your priority. In reality, the only situation I would suggest paying off your house is if the funds come from a *non*-retirement account, like a brokerage account, or if you have the cash lying around.

You Are Better Prepared Than You Think.

In case I didn't say this more succinctly before, I want to make it loud and clear that if you have $200K in savings at retirement age, you may very well be in better shape than you realize. You are not a government statistic. In fact, you may be on a path to a happy retirement.

My hope is that I've shown you that the common assumptions and beliefs many of us hold just don't stand to reason. There is not a retirement crisis in the way the media presents it, and it doesn't apply to you anyway. As I have said before, you don't need a million in the bank to retire, unless you have expectations of an extravagant lifestyle. You can invest in the stock market quite happily post-retirement. It's OK to spend some of the money you saved for retirement, as soon as you retire.

I am not revealing any big investment secrets. My intention is to show you, with data and statistics, that you may have enough not just to retire, but to enjoy retirement without fear and anxiety. Let's go ahead and replace fear and feelings of scarcity with empowerment and financial peace.

Plan, Invest, LIVE Life!

Hear ye, Baby Boomers: by and large you are not going to run out of money in retirement. You have multiple income streams assuming you have your defined benefit plan, and most all you have Social Security.

It is my belief, that if you have your $200,000 invested, with a financial plan in place, you are unlikely to spend away your retirement. I really want to hone in on this point, because the financial fruits that will result from your smart, informed retirement planning are far bigger than the fears that hold you back. I get the fear of the unknown. I'm here to show you how straightforward it is to plan smart for your post-work life.

You can have both safety-net money and spend money.

I want you to replace your financial fear with financial empowerment. We will override fear through knowledge. Get ready to let out a huge sigh of relief. If you are already prepared for retirement, with ample savings, please let that sigh be loud enough for all to hear. If you are not as prepared as you might need to be, you are still going to feel better—because you are taking the first step of *taking charge* of your retirement. You are not going to go broke in retirement. You may be in better financial shape than you realize.

CHAPTER THREE:

But, But...What If, What If

There is nothing stable in the world — uproar
is your only music.
John Keats, 1795-1821

I magine a well-dressed and highly educated woman comes into my office for a consultation. Her work schedule is so grueling that she can only meet in the evenings. I wonder why she has to work so hard—at 67—that she could not make an appointment for earlier in the day.

I ask her the same questions I have learned to ask all new clients about age, marital status, details of existing retirement, savings, and investment accounts, expectations, needs and dreams. She has almost $2 million in investments, no children or spouse, and no interest in passing on her money to other family members. I ask her when she is going to start spending her money.

Her eyes widen. Her face is frozen in an expression of confusion. She looks at me like I have lost my mind. "I can't spend my money," she says sincerely. "If I do, I might run out. What if the stock market drops?"

I've heard the same thing over and over again. Intelligent, thoughtful people who had been working their entire lives, who consider "Wall Street" and "the stock market" mysterious entities.

To her, and many others, the stock market might just as well be a spinning roulette wheel. If I were to ask if the market was up or down last year, most wouldn't know. And if they do, they most likely don't know by how much.

Again, this was a very bright woman with a significant amount of money in play. If this individual lacked a basic understanding of investments and did not have a historical perspective about how the market works, how could I expect anyone else to comprehend it?

What makes educated, intelligent people be so fearful? What could have us so irrationally pessimistic? How can we believe we are in financial shambles (even when we are in better shape than 90 percent of our peers)?

Why does someone with a well-diversified, well-managed portfolio believe that the sky is falling … that their money could be gone at any moment?

My goal is to uncover the answers to these questions and use that information to better your life. It may be possible for you to live a life so much better than you can imagine, and I want to help uncover that reality.

The What If Record Keeps Skipping

Just as myths and beliefs hold us back, we also paralyze our financial optimism by hitting up against the "What If" hurdles.

What if I get sick?
What if a tree falls on my house?
What if World War III happens?

I hear these questions frequently. They are all valid concerns. The world is complex and often unpredictable, so technically, anything *could* happen. That doesn't necessarily mean that these things *will* happen.

I don't mean to take these objections lightly, so instead, let's review the What Ifs.

#1: "What if my portfolio doesn't keep up with inflation."

You're right. You *do* need to consider inflation. Things get more expensive over time. Thirty years from now, a gallon of milk might be $10. One retiree I know quipped to me, "Peanut butter is going to cost so much I'm going to have to end up working at McDonalds."

My father has been an investment advisor for 45 years. I'm approaching two decades into my career. Over the course of our experiences, we've found that the reality is that yes, as you get older, things will become more expensive. However, as you get older you will naturally spend less. In our 60s people tend to spend the most money. In our 70s, folks tend to spend less. In our 80s and 90s, spending typically goes down dramatically.

What happens is a very interesting concept, but age and inflation offset each other. Inflation is rising, your spending is falling. The money you have is staying in your own hands. If you've been spending in check with your budget, and have your retirement savings appropriately invested, then you should be fine.

It's true that we are living longer than ever before, and therefore will have longer retirements than prior generations. Or, at least, it is a very real possibility. Assuming you invest in a manner that protects you from long-term inflationary pressures. By long term, I mean at least three decades from your retirement date. Some of your retirement income is already protected from insurance; namely, your social security payments. I go into more detail in Part Two about this topic.

Inflationary pressures vary on different goods and services and some expenses, like medical care, have become more expensive relative to the increase of other goods and services. For this reason, the Consumer Price Index (CPI), which is how we track the cost of living within the U.S., has created a inflation tracker specific to those over the age of 62. It's call the CPI-E and you can view it on the Bureau of Labor Statistics website.[17] Tracking the cost of the items retirees typically spend more of their income on, namely housing, food, transportation and healthcare, is a good way to keep a tabs on how your portfolio is keeping up with your expenses. This would be a job for your advisor; you'll be updating your budget each year and observing changes to your monthly expenses accordingly.

I've never seen inflation put a retired person in a desperate situation deep into their retirement. The inflation rate has been steadily declining since the 1990s, so the value of your dollar isn't going to drastically drop any time soon. Your generation has been around long enough to remember the hyperinflation era in the 1980s, and so it's natural to worry about inflation. While hyperinflation seems very unlikely, and is difficult to plan against, you can make plans to prepare your portfolio for "normal" inflation (i.e. Invest your retirement savings in the stock market according to a sensible asset allocation plan.)

#2 *"What if I get hit with big medical costs?*

Do medical costs go way up when you retire? Do you require more prescriptions, more office visits? And, what if I need some sort of surgery or I have a heart attack or I have arthritis and I need all kinds of treatment? Eighty percent of Boomers over age 65 have a chronic disease that requires management,[18] so this is not an unreasonable question. It's safe to say that Boomers will reshape the U.S. healthcare system.

A very nice woman, who was about to retire, once told me that she didn't plan on ever spending any of her savings and investments. When I inquired as to why, she said, "I worry about medical costs. There is a history of cancer in my family."

I told her if she enrolled in Medicare and had a Medicare supplement, the most she would have to pay out-of-pocket is $10,000 a year ($6,700 for in-network, at the time of writing).[19] Even if she got cancer and had a $400,000 medical bill, she would be responsible for her deductible only.

Without that tiny tidbit of information, this woman would have made every financial decision for the rest of her life based on a faulty understanding of the facts. She would have lived small, worried about money, and feared the future instead of allowing herself to enjoy it.

At age 65, you qualify for Medicare. A decent Medicare supplement currently costs between $150 and $250 a month. A Medicare supplement covers many of the things that standard Medicare does not, including the so-called "gap" in coverage.

In a worst-case scenario, if you have some sort of traumatic medical issue that requires extensive medical treatment, and you have hospital bills that are $150,000, the general reality is that your out-of-pocket expense is the amount of your Medicare deductible.

Now this is not my specialty, but again, I know the reality, which is medical experiences in retirement often are not a big deal. If you need cataract surgery, Medicare covers a majority of it. Granted, you will have to spend a little bit more money on medications as you get older. Perhaps you'll need new and stronger glasses. Or hearing aids. But if you prepare for these items as part of your retirement spending plan, it should not be the reason why you spend very little when you reach your 60s and 70s.

#3: "What if if I need to go to a nursing home?"

We're all living longer, and questions about long-term care are valid. What if we need a full-service nursing home for 15 years— what happens then? This is the hardest question to answer because we will all be different in how we are impacted by physical and mental health as we age. The cost of long-term care is a legitimate financial issue for our society.

The good news is that most of us will not need a nursing home for the long-term. Morningstar found that just seven percent of women and two percent of men will need nursing home care for more than five years.[20] That's a relatively small portion of the population who will run into a situation where they have an extended long-term care stay.

Long-term care is very expensive. The average private room in a nursing home will run you around $92K a year.[21] Home care workers and nurses are a much less expensive route to getting the care we need in our elder years, when family members are not in a position to help, or need support to care for their loved ones.

Still, the long-term care fear is absolutely overblown. It is a reality. It's a real thing to consider, but it is not a reason to live in fear.

Consider someone who tells me, "Dave, I have $500,000, but I'm not going to spend any of it because you never know. I might end up in a nursing home."

Is this really the way we want to live? Do we want to live the rest of our lives in fear, waiting to live in a nursing home when there is a low chance that we're going to actually live there for a long time and deplete our savings?

Plan for the worst, LIVE like the best will unfold.
The stats are on your side.

You can mitigate the risk of nursing home expenses by buying long-term care insurance. There are tools you can use to protect yourself in case of long-term care bills. It's something that should be explored. I don't want to discount that.

Remember, too, that Medicaid is an option. If you don't have enough money, the government will pay for long-term care through Medicaid. Medicare does not cover custodial nursing home care, though it does provide cover time in a skilled nursing facility, providing you were hospitalized for three days prior.[22]

A common concern is what happens if my spouse has to go to a nursing home and I have to spend all my money to provide for them? I may be left with no money and have to live in poverty the rest of my life.

There are government policies in place to protect you in this instance. The reality is that the federal government allows you to keep your house, car and a significant amount of savings. There are simple things you can do to make sure you are not impoverished by a sick spouse. So again, while it's something that needs to be addressed and something that needs to be planned for, it is not a valid reason to never spend any money or to spend a very small amount when you retire.

In the end, you have to make the decision. Do you want to live in fear of something that is improbable, or do you want to live a full life based on assumptions that are realistic? I've met clients who have a philosophy that is summed up by one word: defer.

Defer happiness. Defer gifts to children. Defer the dream of traveling to see the world.

They believe they are required to live a very uninspired life. Clients, when they say to me that they are concerned about medical costs as they get older, are perpetuating a myth. They really haven't spent time talking with someone who knows what the financial realities of retirement are.

I hear the nursing home worry all the time. I get it. There are scary costs associated with long-term care. But if we consider the likelihood of needing long-term care, the options we have to mitigate against the expenses of long-term care, and if we understand how the system actually works, you can still enjoy your retirement while spending smart.

#4: "What if I get scammed?"

It's not just retirees who are concerned about getting scammed. That said, thanks to the fact that most of America's wealth sits with Boomers at the moment, you are a lucrative target for scammers.

While Millennials are more likely to be scammed than those over 70,[23] the reality is that the amount an older person might be scammed for is more—again, because we have more money saved.

There are myriad scams you've likely heard of, and you know to be weary of the hard sell, too-good-to-be-true returns that accompany the "sales pitch" of many scammers. The Federal Trade Commission lists 30 categories of scams ranging from debt collection scams, which take up nearly 23 percent of scams, down to buyer's clubs. What about investment scams? There were 15,079 investment scams reported to the FTC in 2017, making up 0.56 percent of total reported scams.[24]

In the context of grand world of scams, investment scams comprise a surprisingly low number—relatively speaking. Still, when an investment scam does hit, it can be devastating, hence the fear.

The most notorious investment scam of all time is Bernie Madoff's Ponzi scheme, which was outed in 2008. Madoff accepted investor payments directly to his wealth management firm for decades—some say all the way back to the '70s. He provided his clients with high return and actual payouts, all supported by fabricated statements and trade reports. It was all "one big lie," as he reportedly told his son. The payouts to clients simply came from monies provided by new influxes of cash from willing investors—many of which included foundations and hospitals, and even large banks from around the world!

It was only when Madoff admitted his scheme to his sons, and they reported him to the SEC, that his intricate and meticulously-executed scam was unfurled. To this day, I hear from folks who distrust financial advisors as a result of Madoff's fraud of $18 billion (or as much as $65 billion, depending on which account you read).

The key difference between Madoff and your typical advisor is that Madoff accepted the funds *directly,* whereas an advisor usually does not have possession of your assets.

> *Your stocks, bonds and cash should be held by a third-party custodian like an SIPC-insured brokerage firm. Not with your advisor.*

You give permission for your advisor to trade on your behalf, to wire funds to your same name accounts according to your instructions, and to deduct a pre-agreed management fee. No reputable advisor who is working within the law will ever ask you to write a check to them. It's actually *not* illegal for an advisor to start their own bank/custodian; that's what Madoff essentially did. Still, I would advise opting for an advisor who does not hold your assets: the check and balance of the custodian provides protection for both you and your advisor.

So, in short: you are very unlikely to be swindled by the Bernie Madoffs of the world. Investment scams are lower on the fraud list in part thanks to our state and federal regulators like the SEC and FINRA. You should always check your advisor's record on those sites: any complaints are registered, as are crimes or liens on property.

At the top of the scam lists are debt scams, where fraudsters will tell you you owe X dollars and require "repayment." Other scams include identity theft and imposter scams where individuals pretend to be, say, your bank representative, over the phone. There are also newsletter scams that try to convince you to invest in the "deal of a century." You know the type of scams I'm talking about.

There's lots of great information on the AARP site to clue yourself up as to scams, if you want to know more.

In general I say follow the golden rule that you send no money to anyone—no checks, no transfers, no withdrawals. No one other than you needs to gain access to any of your accounts—no sharing passwords or downloading files or software as the result of a phone call or email you receive from a new, helpful "representative."

It might sound elementary, but you'd be surprised at how adept scammers are at getting you to give up passwords or to get you to give access to your accounts. It's unlikely to happen but it doesn't hurt to be in the know. Follow these rules and you won't have to worry about scammers getting into your account. And you certainly shouldn't have to be concerned about scammers getting into your retirement savings if you lock down passwords and access.

But, But

I know. Even when you shut off the *What If* record, a voice in your head calls out, "...but, but!" Your mind is right to go there. Considering the risks is part of making a strategic informed retirement plan.

When you sit down to plan your retirement income, you and your advisor will take into account all the "what if" costs, relative to your specific risk profile, with some breathing room of unanticipated costs.

We account for these expenses in your rainy day fund. And remember, over time, your invested savings should continue to increase. As you enter into your older years and perhaps need more care, you've still got your pension income, your social security income, and Medicaid and Medicare on your side. We have not even begun to tap into your investable assets yet. And it's worth keeping in mind at this point that your expenditures on other things will go down.

You Are Better Protected Than You Think

Absent nuclear destruction and the Great Depression revisited, you are set. Social Security is going to deliver for you. You have pension income and investable assets. You have protections in place and rainy day funds.

Now that we see those *What Ifs* in a new, much less probable light, we can contemplate a more positive view on our retirement. I hope you can contemplate a much more optimistic and colorful retirement than many folks I meet.

It's true for at least half of Boomers that you are:

a) better off than you think
b) better prepared than you think and
c) living in a much less riskier world than you might think.

As we close the chapter, keep these three points in mind:

1. There will always be things that can go wrong, but you will position yourself to be protected and prepared … and you can still spend some of your savings.
2. Understand where your fears come from so that you can take charge of them, investing with strategic optimism.
3. Empower your mindset to accept the income you can afford to take. Your five percent pie slice is yours for the taking. If not yours, then someone else's.

CHAPTER FOUR:

You Know More Than The Media Thinks

Comment is free, but facts are sacred.
CP Scott, 1846-1932

When we are on rough seas, we look for a safe harbor. And those who experience rough seas will never forget the experience. They often spend the rest of their days hugging the shore and staying close to those safe harbors. Whenever we suffer difficulties or a trauma, physical or psychological, we do what we can to avoid a repeat of our suffering.

The same holds true for financial troubles. Hard times teach us ways to weather them: spending out of jars marked "groceries" and "clothing" and avoiding debt sounds like a prudent way to budget, and it is, but never deviating or planning your financial life to live a little? That's heartbreaking, especially in an era of massive wealth creation.

Those who have suffered extreme deprivation in the hardest times didn't simply learn lessons; they earned scars. The generation that lived through the Great Depression in the 1930s never forgot a moment of what that was like. Deprivation, seared into their consciousness, created a distrust of financial institutions. The experience of dispossession resonated long after the Depression.

Sons and daughters who heard the family war stories
of money gained and lost, are now retiring —
with a similar sense of pessimism as their parents.

Why would talking about the Depression and how it affected those who lived through it be relevant to our discussion of retirement and the Boomer Generation? Your upbringing imprints an indelible stamp on you. And if Depression-era parents reared you, you may well have been born into a family whose relationship with financial institutions and money was unpredictable at best.

If you are a Baby Boomer, chances are that you have the not-so-subconscious financial traits that were passed down to you by parents who saw people lose everything, who saw people go hungry, and who saw firsthand the crushing weight of poverty. Over the years, within this cohort of Baby Boomers raised by children of the Depression, I have recognized a palpable doubt that money, which they have worked prudently for and judiciously saved, will be there when they need it.

Baby Boomers created a world of massive development. Technological development meant that we had the new gadgets and gizmos, and the post World War II boom meant we had lots to make, and lots to buy. What did we all buy? Televisions. Baby Boomers were the first generation to be raised with television. Inevitably came the commercials. Now, not only did Boomers have their neighbors to compare themselves to, but also the rest of America, specifically the upper middle sections of the population.

Boomers have made more money than any generation, yet they don't believe they have enough to be comfortable in life or retirement.

A Depression-era mentality
+ unparalleled economic growth
+ a whole new level of keeping up with the Joneses
= a complicated headspace to live in.

Our fears and desires are played on in the name of selling us stuff we may or may not need—that includes financial vehicles that don't have your best interests at heart.

Enter the Fear Mongers

The Depression-era mindset makes retirement planning tricky enough, but we also have to contend with advertisers and salespeople who play to our fears, with unsound advice designed not to make retirement safer but to make the fear mongers richer.

For example, currently there is a unique, alarmist cry on our televisions that preys on the psychology of Boomers who have most internalized the fearful mindset of their Depression-era parents. This is the cry to invest in silver and gold.

I have become something of an informal student of these scare tactics. From print ads to late-night television commercials, I have studied these investment opportunities and have been fascinated, disturbed, and even outraged by their blatant appeals to uncertainties and fear. The only explanation I have for Boomers being unable to see through the noise is their family history as children of their Depression-era parents.

How do these ads play out? They start with the presumption that "only precious metals are permanent" and that governments that are printing money ("worthless paper") are generally untrustworthy. They follow with the claim that the economy continues to be as bad, or worse, than 2007 when the stock market fell. While I would argue that the case they make is questionable at best, their ads are remarkably effective.

Their presentation usually follows a line of reasoning that goes something like this:

We're facing huge, HUGE financial problems in the United States. If you thought 2008 was bad, you haven't seen anything yet.

Government statistics are lies. Falling unemployment rate? Who're you kidding? People are out of work. The government is making up the numbers. "Real" unemployment is 30 percent or more.

The Fed is manipulating interest rates and our economy.

Oil and commodities are tanking.

We are maybe on the precipice of another stock market bubble.

Our national debt is out of control. When the government needs more money, it just prints it. And things will only get worse.

But act quickly… because tomorrow may be too late!

Take, for example, a 2017 article in Barron's: "Be Afraid: Dow Drops 100 Points as Bears Maul Bulls."[25] Now, I consider Barron's to be a credible, mainstream business journal but titles like the one above practically invite readers to freak out. With fear-mongering statements such as "A strong open was too good to last," the article painted a portrait of doom and gloom.

Here are some other panic-inducing articles I've seen:

- *"The Imminent Stock Market Crash" (ProfitConfidential.com - April 8, 2016)*[26]
- *"We Have Just Witnessed a 'Death Cross' in the Market's Fear Indicator" (Yahoo.com - March 10, 2016)*[27]
- *"This Will Make the Next Stock Market Crash as Bad as 2008" (WallStreetExaminer.com - March 9, 2016)*[28]
- *"Here's Another Sign a Recession is Coming." (Fortune.com - March 29, 2016)*[29]

Headlines like those above frighten investors. They exasperate us too. I can't tell you how many clients come in unnerved by the latest Doomsday headline. Even the most rational, intelligent and informed of us feel unsettled by these headlines, and it's natural to feel this way.

"The talking heads are saying the markets are going nuts. Will the Fed increase interest rates? Will the price of oil rise? Are we facing the next Great Recession?"—this line of questioning is common in my office.

I have seen the same news programs and have become incensed enough to shout at the television, a habit that causes my wife to shake her head patiently while she gestures toward the children to pay no attention to Daddy.

Hundreds of articles like the ones above are published every month. And there have been thousands of articles published like this every year for the past 20 years. And what has the stock market done for the past 20 years? From 1995 through 2015, the stock market has had an average annual return of—you guessed it—10 percent.

Hey, Chicken Little...the Sky is *Not* Falling

It's not just the late night ads, but also the drive of the 24-hour news cycle that helps feed the market fear frenzy. The news, with its need to be compelling and to keep you tuned in, is often sensational and almost always contradictory. The questions and confusion only adds to a feeling of angst. And with or without the news, hourly tracking of the Dow Jones would make anyone crazy.

No one trusts the stock market. No one trusts the banks. They mistrust the financial system itself, even though many would be hard pressed to describe what it is, exactly.

It is so troubling to me that we, as a population, use overdramatic news broadcasts as our sources of information. We're essentially changing the courses of our lives—and sometimes limiting ourselves—by listening to sensationalistic financial news reports, and making overly fear-based decisions about spending and investing as a result.

In our minds, the ability to pay the costs of living and live a sensible retirement is directly related to the ups and downs of the stock market. The stock market itself is not necessarily representative of the overall economy: only 52 percent of Americans are invested in the stock market, and less than one percent of America's 27 million businesses are traded on the stock market.[30] Nobel prize winning economist Paul Samuelson is popularly quoted as saying, "The stock market has forecast nine of the last five recessions." That is to the say the stock market moves according to investors' expectations about the future economy—and seeing as humans are behind those decisions, those beliefs can be downright wrong. Stocks go up and down, sometimes with good cause, and sometimes with no apparently sane reasoning.

The sky is not falling, so don't let the 24/7 news cycle convince you otherwise.

It is mind-boggling to me to think about the emotional turmoil Dow surfers must suffer daily. Yes, the stock market dropped six percent last week. So what?

I believe that you should never get caught up in the daily, weekly or monthly rise and fall of the stock market, especially without understanding all of its variables. Doing so is a recipe for needless anxiety.

The reality is that, since World War II, the S&P 500 has only been down 15 times (in the last 75 years).[31]

Even during the 2008 recession, during which it dipped significantly as a result of the housing crisis, the market not only recovered, but by 2017 increased to a surprising level: from 7,889.20 in February 2009 to more than 20,000 points in a period of seven years.

In the 1980s, the Keating scandal drew the market down. And in October 1987, the market dropped. In early 2018, the market went into a free fall for no apparent reason, and then turned back around—unemployment was the lowest in 17 years, and consumer and business confidence were at record levels, so there didn't appear to be a good reason. Volatility happens; just as we work with changes in the weather, when we understand that the sun comes out after the storm.

The market corrects itself over time, which is why it is a savvier approach to consider what the market has returned *over time*. We are going to talk more about historical perspective in Chapter 7.

Media Proof Your Retirement Mindset

There was a time when people who dealt with finances for a living recognized that the market, like the weather, was going to have good stretches and bad. And the wise thing to do was to hunker down during the bad ones and enjoy the good. Adopt the long-view mindset and think of losses as temporary, and gains as permanent. (And when I say temporary losses, I mean temporary "unrealized" losses—because we don't sell just because the market dips; we typically stay the course, positioned to embrace the gains that time and time again typically follow.)

Unfortunately, it seems our investing culture no longer has as much patience or understanding of the long view. A few decades ago, most of us were invested in the market through fixed corporate pension plans. Today, most of us are individually invested in the stock market. That means we are all watching the market news, with varying degrees of sophistication and experience. The financial media machine has conditioned people to react to short-term fluctuations and thrives on making people market-trigger-happy on a minute-by-minute basis. As a populace, we are jumpy. Acting on fear, rather than reason.

Buy now! Sell before it's too late! Sections of the media have created a frenzy. Millions of people believe in the core of their being that, if they don't buy or sell at exactly the right moment, they will have jeopardized their financial well-being for the rest of their lives.

That, my friends, is not true.

I believe it is a destructive lie not just because it causes people to worry, lose sleep and suffer various physical ailments, but because it convinces them that they cannot and should not spend some of their retirement savings during retirement.

Successful investing is about TIME IN the market,
not TIMING the market.

Dishonest statements about the stock market stream into our consciousness through many means—social media, email marketing and video sites, to names a few sources. Increasingly so, doomsday market pros—so-called advisors who make money based on you buying financial products—email you with carefully crafted, fear-laden sales copy to convince you that they will protect you from market volatility and the freefalls they predict with so much non-science.

Quick reality check: no one knows what the stock market will do for certain. No one. The Fed doesn't know. I don't know. Anyone who says they do know should be heard with a grain of salt.

Clickbait is another popular technique used by financial fearmongers in the Internet age—clickbait is internet content that is designed to direct you to a specific website, which, in turn, sells you a product, or tries to convince you of the author's agenda. It's the Internet's version of "yellow journalism"—unresearched, unverified and unsupported news led with a catchy headline that usually has the intention to sell you on something.

The technique works like this: write something so outrageous, scary or shocking that you can't help but notice. The content is dressed in dramatic phrases to pull you in with the purpose of getting you to click through and buy.

Once they get you to click, you are hit with their "news article" (a.k.a. fear- mongering content designed to sell you something you don't need). It might look official and legitimate, but it is just an advertisement for different financial companies or news outlets.

If so many of my clients need near-daily reassurance that their retirement is safe, and that no, they don't need to subscribe to these attention-seeking newsletters, there must be other people across the country like them who are suffering just as much.

It is time for a *radical* transformation in the way Baby Boomers and soon-to-be retirees live their lives, and view their investing habits and their retirement savings. But I cannot tell you how hard the unethical sections of the financial media will fight against such a transformation. They will fight because they have a lot to lose if Boomers don't buy into their constant "The sky-is-falling!" rants.

Even some financial advisors and money managers will push back against a change in the paradigm, but a change is necessary—if Boomers are going to enjoy their retirements and use their hard-earned savings and investments wisely and to their maximum benefit.

Boomers, do not confuse short term with long term. Do not listen to the fear mongers. Don't hide your money in your mattress. Trust your prudent, diversified investments. Enjoy your retirement. As you will soon learn, it is much simpler than you would think.

Know How to Identify the Good from the Bad.

There *is*, of course, reasoned media out there, but it is not necessarily speaking to you. The market will fluctuate; there will always be corrections as investors absorb new information. We know by now to trust in the long-term performance of our thoughtfully constructed portfolios. Media scaremongers need not try to convince you otherwise, but they will try. When they do, you'll spot it and laugh it off, safe in the knowledge that you know better.

All that said, I cannot say with 100 percent certainty that we will never have another Great Depression. Do I think it at all likely? No. If there is a one percent chance of economic disaster, do you really want to live your life in that one percent space? Wouldn't you rather put your money on the 99 percent chance that we will continue to live in the most affluent time in all of human history? Wouldn't you rather enjoy that 99 percent chance that technology will continue to make life easier, more enjoyable and more fascinating? Wouldn't you rather live in that 99 percent space where you do the things you love to do?

If you take away anything from this chapter, let it be these three things:

1. The media can get over-excited when the market moves. Fear tactics and "alternative facts" are designed to target your vulnerabilities. There are reasoned discussions and opinions available. Ask yourself: does the author benefit from their message—are they ultimately selling me a product like a newsletter?

2. Armed with historical perspective, and a clearer picture of your retirement preparedness, you can switch off the talking heads with a good conscience.

3. Have faith. Trust your prudent, diversified portfolio. Listen to your advisor (assuming they don't jump every time the media says to!).

CHAPTER FIVE:

It's Time for the Investment Industry to Shift

*It is difficult to get a man to understand something, when
his salary depends upon his not understanding it!*
Upton Sinclair, 1878-1968

When you think of the investment industry—Wall Street,
banks, insurance—what comes to mind? I'm guessing
that you don't feel warm and fuzzy. And that the words "trust,"
"integrity" and "my best interests" are not exactly sitting on the tip
of your tongue.

Given the industry's well-reported history of misconduct and
profiteering, I don't blame people for judging my industry harshly.
It's a weight I carry as an investment professional, though I do
believe that there are many, many ethical and caring investment
advisors serving clients in this country.

Now, this chapter is not about purported crooks of Wall
Street; we've all heard the stories and frankly it would take up the
whole book.

In this chapter, we will talk about a conflict of interest that could hold advisors back from advising you to spend your retirement savings. We will also talk about some of the different conflicts of interest that can affect investors, and which types of conflict apply to some advisors more than others. My goal is for you to put this information in your financial toolbox, to help you select an advisor aligned with your best interests.

An advisor can be driven by integrity, and still have a conflict of interest, whether they like it or not. We have good people in the investment industry who are operating with the best of intentions, putting into practice their company's training with little questioning as to whether the status quo of their investment advice is truly in their clients' best interests.

To know your best interests, your advisor needs to know you—what you want to accomplish with your money. You don't amount to black and red numbers on your statements, and your advisor's advice should reflect that understanding.

I believe that one of your advisor's fundamental goals should be for you to have funds not just for a rainy day, but for living the life you dream of—to maximize the potential of your savings for spending in retirement. What's it for, if not to be used for your best life? Not everyone agrees with me.

In the Business of Growing Money. Period.

Early in my career, I sat down with a new client. She told me about her life. In a job like mine, you hear a lot about people's highs and lows, because, at the end of the day, your financial well-being is connected to your life's whole picture. In her case, she was in her mid 60s, and she had some serious health issues.

Her marriage didn't work out and she opted not to marry again. She didn't have children or any close relatives. She had about $200,000 in a retirement account.

As we talked, she mentioned that she was retiring. I told her I thought that was a good move. After all, she was of an age when many people retired, and her company pension and Social Security were able to satisfy her budget needs. So I asked her when she was going to start using the money in her retirement savings account.

She looked at me funny and shrugged. Just like the folks in my Social Security class I told you about in Chapter 1, she assumed that she would take the money out "when she needed it." And her reply sounded more like a question than a statement.

"You've worked hard to save this money," I told her. "You should use it for what you saved it for: to *enjoy your retirement*. You have plenty saved for life's hiccups and elder-year needs, and you have a solid recurring income from your Social Security and pension plan."

She thought for a moment and then nodded her head. It made a lot of sense to her. So, I started sending her some money each month. Not a lot of money. A prudent, sustainable amount. In fact, it equaled the amount of interest her retirement savings was earning. Nothing more. But it was a few dollars that she enjoyed.

I spoke with a fellow advisor, who was a peer mentor to me, about the approach. He was a 20-year veteran in the business, and he looked at me like I just didn't "get it."

I know you are new in this business," he said, "so take some advice from someone who has built up a healthy book of business: don't tell your clients to spend their money. It is going to cost you big time over your career."

My friend was not in any way vindictive or looking to hurt his clients. He loved his clients. He was convinced that keeping as much money invested as possible was prudent; his clients having more funds invested also happened to be more beneficial to him. He was attracted to the business primarily to make money, period; rather than making money to fulfill a purpose.

"You've got to keep building up the assets you are managing. The more assets your clients have to invest, the more your annual fees will stack up. *Everyone* makes more money that way."

I felt, in that moment, like the real goal in making money was being lost. We can collect numbers of anything. What is the meaning behind *only* making money—is money not the tool? It's a vehicle to life experience, and security. Isn't the point of investments to give clients extra money to use for life's surprises, but also to enjoy? What do we invest for if not to be prepared for life and to live a little?

"We are in the business of helping people grow their money and accumulate wealth." Note the period after "wealth." There is no "... in order to help people live out their dreams" or "...to enjoy life as they see fit" following "accumulate wealth." Not from this guy.

Why is it only the job of the advisor to grow money and keep it in the account, accumulating and compounding in perpetuity? One simple reason: financial institutions are compensated by how much money is in the client's account, not by how much goes out from the account. It sounds elementary and fair, but in truth it's troubling.

We Fee-based Advisors Have Fewer Conflicts than Others, but We Still Have One.

Fee-only models are supposed to avoid the conflicts of interest commission-paid brokers have (we'll talk more about the impact of commissions shortly), but as our story above shows, you can't completely avoid conflicts of interest. A fee-only advisor is incentivized to invest as much of your money as possible, as we get paid on the amount you have invested. Of course, fee-only investment advisors have a fiduciary responsibility to you and we all must follow SEC rules to put your best interests first.

While many advisors do an admirable job at creating diversified asset allocation strategies for their clients, what they often don't do, in my opinion, is create plans that allow retirees to *use* and enjoy their money.

If we don't question the idea that we should not spend during retirement, the status quo of growing portfolios without spending sounds great. Fee-based advisors get paid on a percentage, often one percent, of that ever-growing, never-spent portfolio. The fee is not unfair, per se; it's just that I believe honest and capable advisors can subconsciously fall into the trap of not encouraging you to stay invested, rather than spending.

This "preserve the client's accumulated capital" philosophy is a real challenge in the financial services industry—as it is in an advisor's best interest to sometimes go against what may be in the best interest of a firm's clients. Merely due to the inherent way that we are paid.

Now, I am not suggesting for a second that the industry does not need or deserve to be compensated for financial management advice. What I am suggesting is that there is an inherent bias baked into the process that could affect the kind of advice an advisor gives to a client. By telling a client to take money from his or her account, we are very literally taking money from our pockets, and the pockets of our managers, if we work for a larger practice. That was the lesson my peer in the story above wanted me to learn.

The math is clear. With less money in the account, there is less revenue for the advisor, and the advisor's institution receives less income.

When we ask retirees today, "When are you going to start using your money? And when you do, how much are you going to use each month?" My belief is that maybe one out of ten have an answer. I've asked people this questions and mostly, I am met with blank stares and confused looks. They're not used to hearing questions about actually spending in retirement. Unfortunately, there are a lot of financial advisors who don't think you should spend your savings once you retire. I can tell this by the number of eyebrows I see jumping as I meet with folks on the cusp of retiring, or who have already retired.

More often than not, I have found that my industry ends up doing a poor job helping retirees create a plan of attack to get the most life from their money. For all the benefits the Boomers have enjoyed, when it comes to their retirement investments, they're getting hit from all sorts of strange directions. Not only are they carrying the psychological burden of their Depression-era parents and the relentless fear-mongering of the financial media, they also have to overcome the inherently selfish designs of the financial industry. It's no wonder people stumble blindly through this process.

In my view, advisors should be telling clients:

- *Invest your portfolio so you can use and enjoy the money you've worked so hard to save.*
- *Get the most cash in your pockets during the years you are going to enjoy it most, without mortgaging your future.*

You have spent a lifetime working and saving, investing wisely and looking forward to your retirement. I believe you deserve to benefit from your money as you enjoy that retirement—and that the advisor's role is to make your investments serve your saving and spending goals.

If that means travel, then I want that money to allow you to travel. If that means assisting charities, then I want you to have the money to do that. If that means sending your grandson to a special summer camp in Colorado, then I want you to do that. If that means buying a family vacation cabin in the mountains, then do that. If it means taking up bungee-jumping then hey, go for it.

Conflicts of Interest are so Serious, they are up for Legal Debate.

It was no shock to me when the Department of Labor's "Fiduciary Rule" was scheduled to come into law in June 2018, after eight years of development. At the time of this book's publishing, the rule, unpopular in the broker-dealer world, has been put on hold. But here's why the Fiduciary Rule matters: it's trying to make all investment advisory professionals *have* to give investment advice *that is in the best interests of the clients.*

It may come as a surprise, but there are many thousands of investment advisors that do not automatically fall into the category of a fiduciary.

A fiduciary is a person who is required by law to provide investment advice that is in the best interests of their clients. You'll know your advisor is a fiduciary because they will be registered with the SEC or their applicable state, and categorized as an "RIA"— Registered Investment Advisor. RIAs are compensated by a percentage of fees, based on the assets held in the account, usually around one percent. Some brokers, on the other hand, are paid commissions by the funds and financial products they recommend.

If your advisor is incentivized to recommend funds, you can argue that they may choose the funds that pay *them* the most, with their fees potentially taking away from your principal and return. As long as they are recommending a product that is "roughly suitable" to you, without the Fiduciary Rule, they are working within the law. The Fiduciary Rule wanted to put that conflict of interest to bed. The industry argued that fewer investment products would be available should the rule come to force.

Conflicted advice can mean retirees have been stripped of at least some of their spending money, before we even talk about actually spending.

The non-partisan Economic Policy Institute recently released a study of the impact of conflicted investment advice; they suggest that conflicted advice costs retirement savers some $17B a year.[32] Their stats relate to advisors who gain commissions for brokering certain products to you. That means that your investment has paid your advisor a commission that you can't necessarily see on your statements. We talk about not spending in retirement, but an additional concern for you and your savings is the potential spending money you lost in undisclosed fees and commissions, and that's before you consider the impact of compounded returns on your growing wealth in the first place.

Of course, there are plenty of integrity-driven brokers who want to do the right thing by you. At the end of the day, however, I believe the business model they have entered into derives its success by them doing the right thing for themselves. Many brokerages are reducing their fees as a result of the publicity related to the rule, and the investing public's growing understanding of the conflicts of interests that affect them. But, I believe, we have further to go as an industry to do the right thing by the investing public. We also have to do better, as an industry, to help investors have a sense that their advisor works for the clients, and not the creators of financial products, first and foremost.

I'm sure many advisors would argue that they are telling you not to spend so that you don't run out of money in your 80s and 90s, and I am happy to debate with them the legitimacy of their concern. They are acting as your prudent fiduciary by investing for a long retirement. But let's be real: There is no fiduciary rule or other law that is going to incentivize or require an advisor to advise you to spend more. It's not in our best interests, and many may convincingly argue it's not in your best interest. Depending on where you sit on the caution spectrum, you'll agree with the overcautious conservative advisors, or you'll agree with me—the "let's get the most LIFE out of your MONEY" advisor.

There's a Shift Coming...

The investment industry is going through a shift, and it's about time. It's going through a shift in addressing conflicts of interest and meeting the best interests of clients. It's also going through a shift in its messaging thanks to Baby Boomers. Your generation really knows how to disrupt the status quo.

Retirement planning commercials are beginning to focus more on the life you want to lead than they did when I started out. Marketing is one thing, but what happens in practice? The same compensation mechanisms are in place as before, and thus the same incentives. Still, there is a change in tone coming from the banks and investment firms, at least in terms of their communications. By putting out ads that reflect Baby Boomers' higher expectations, they are inviting a conversation from you. So hold them accountable; tell them what you want and ask them how they are going to tailor your portfolio beyond risk tolerance.

How are they going to help you spend for a great retirement as you save for the necessities in the elder years? We advisors are up to the challenge.

Many advisors feel the way I do. And I have come to learn that the vast majority of retiring Baby Boomers cannot do this work on their own. You need an objective and caring professional to help expertly guide and direct your finances through this time in your life. When retirees face decisions that are financial, and emotional, and require complex and intellectually demanding strategies, finding an expert reduces the pressure. It's why professional athletes have managers and agents, and why a small business turns to a CPA to navigate preparing profit-and-loss reports.

It's fascinating for me to hear all the different stories of my clients. Some of them have been teachers, others architects, engineers, people from all different walks of life. They all had different ideals and goals, so it's satisfying and rewarding for me to help them get there. I really do feel blessed by my line of work. In the process, I've learned a lot about what other advisors are telling their clients, and one of the things I've learned is that it is easy to "lose the forest for the trees."

We all get so caught up in in how we allocate our investment—60 percent in bonds? 55 percent? Small cap? How much should we have in international companies? What about annuities? How much should we have in cash? How much should we have in real estate? This list goes on and on. What do you think about the Chinese currency? What about the latest election result? Is it time to buy Apple stock? The buzzwords and company names are flying with numbers and statistics being tossed left and right. It's enough to make you crazy!

All these questions really do is muddy the waters. At the end of the day, instead of asking these questions we should start with the presumption that this money is to be used. Money that only exists on a sheet of paper is useless. Your investment means nothing if you only look at the bottom line and stress about growing it indefinitely. If I identified the biggest problem with the financial industry, it would be that we financial advisors spend almost all of our time talking about risk tolerance, investments, asset allocations, performance and stock market cycles at the expense of *why* we are investing in the first place.

Yes, all these other issues are important. They are part of what makes and keeps your retirement investments healthy. But in the larger scheme of things, they are the smaller part. The most important thing is, how do we translate these investments—these scratches on a piece of paper—into a tool to affect our lives?

What do we want our investments to do for us? How we can put our investments to work to make ourselves, and the people we love, happy, and to support issues we care about, while we are here?

Ultimately, before you can form any plan for your retirement, you have to give some thought to what you want your retirement to be. Think about your genuine, deep passions. Have you always wanted to visit India? Do you want to play golf every day?

Do you want to be a strong supporter of your church or community? Do you want to spend more time with your grandchildren?

What does your money mean to you? In reality, there is no great truth about the meaning of money. It all depends on you. We're going to dive deep into this in Part Three. First, we will dive into the nuts and bolts of budgets, Social Security planning and keeping your historical perspective in check. Keep in mind, though, the true foundation of retirement planning: defining what makes for a meaningful retirement.

If you remember three things from this chapter.

1. An advisor is not financially incentivized to tell you to spend, but they might be philosophically. Make sure you are aligned with your advisor when it comes to strategies for spending as well as saving.

2. There are two types of advisor: Those who have to act in *your* best interests and those who only have to provide "roughly suitable" advice. In my opinion, an advisor who is also considered a fiduciary is your best ally in preparing for retirement.

3. Before we talk risk tolerance and asset allocation, consider your dreams, wants and values. How do you want to put your investment income to work?

PART TWO

CHAPTER SIX:

What Do You Really Want?

But it is pretty to see what money will do.
Samuel Pepys, 1633-1703

In Part Two, we are going to talk about how to create your retirement plan. But before we do, there is one question I want you to start asking yourself: what do you really want from your retirement?

When it comes down to it, your money is there to help you have the most fulfilling retirement possible. It's a bit of a "chicken and the egg" problem. To know how much you will need, you have to have a good idea about what a meaningful retirement means to you. In order to know what kind of life you can have in retirement, you need to know what your financial situation will be.

The reason you are doing this planning work is so that you can have the best retirement for you. You need to have meaning behind this task, not to be driven by fear and worry. Be driven by your desire for informed optimism and the ability to make choices about how you will live your best retirement, whatever that looks like for you specifically.

Ultimately, before you can form any plan for your retirement, you have to give some thought to what you want your retirement to be. Think about your genuine, deep passions.

I have spoken with people who retired with $5 million in their retirement accounts and lived less satisfying retirements than someone who retired with $500,000. Why? Because the trick to a meaningful retirement is how you use your money, not how much you have.

What does your money mean to you? In reality, there is no great truth about the meaning of money. It all depends on you. This is your money after all. High six figures on your balance sheet can certainly be comforting. Seeing $900,000, for example, looks great, but unless—and until—you translate that number into a reality, whatever comfort you find in the number is illusory. It might be too little for one person, or a mind-blowing amount to another. For any person, it's more than you need for the basics and healthcare expenses. It's enough to officially commit to banishing fear and worry from your mindset. Even $200,000 is enough to have anxiety stricken from your connection to money.

A Word About Assumptions

Before we go forward, I want to be clear that my five percent spend plan is based on some assumptions.

1. You have saved at least $200K.
2. You've invested (or will soon invest) your savings in a diversified portfolio of stocks and bonds with at least half of your investable funds in stocks.

If you don't have savings of at least $200K, you can still absolutely use the information in Part Two. The five percent spend rule might not apply as liberally, but the retirement budget planning and Social Security information should be of service to you.

What I am not saying:
1. I'm not telling you to go blow your retirement savings.
2. We are not going to mortgage your retirement.

My intention IS to:
1. Give you the most bang for *your* retirement buck.
2. Show that most people wait *way* too long to starting spending.

I'll show you how you can start spending now.

As a financial advisor, if a 25-year-old comes into my office and asks me, "Dave, can you be my advisor and help me grow this money until I retire?" I just tell them, "No. All you need to do is put your money into a stock-based mutual fund. You want to invest it in the stock market. You want to save as much as you can. And don't think about it until you're 55 or 60! It's not overly simplistic. That's all you need to do."

But once people retire, that advice changes. Suddenly the gravity of your financial situation ratchets up considerably. No longer are you working and making an income. Now you are relying on your savings to support your lifestyle for 20 or more years. Perfectly rational and intelligent people suddenly start making emotionally-charged decisions. Emotion and investing make for a terrible combination.

I know people nearing retirement or who are already retired who need a competent financial advisor in their lives, because it is nearly impossible to successfully navigate through retirement on your own from an investing *and* planning standpoint. So, we will start to talk about exactly how that looks, how you can go from where you are now, and turn it into your best life possible.

It's all about creating a plan that will allow you to find that balance between never running out of money and living your best life NOW.

I often see people set budgets without really knowing how much they have to spend. If they need any extra money, they withdraw as little as possible from their retirement accounts to get by. It shouldn't work that way. It should work the opposite way. You need to let the *total* of *your portfolio* tell you how much you can spend each month.

You've earned a magnificent retirement. Let's make sure you live accordingly. Ready?

Let's roll.

CHAPTER SEVEN:

Hey, Market Drama!
Meet Historical Perspective

Forecasts may tell you a great deal about the forecaster;
they tell you nothing about the future.
Warren Buffett

D o you remember when you first learned how to drive? I know
you are probably wondering what learning to drive has to do
with retirement, but stick with me, just for a minute.

My dad taught me how to drive. And like an awful lot of other
subjects my dad taught me, there was a lot to learn. When I first got
behind the wheel and started the car, I thought I was ready. I was so
anxious to start driving that I couldn't get my permit fast enough.

Making sure there was no traffic, he had me ease the car away
from the curb and start to drive. I found myself constantly jerking
the steering wheel to the left and the right to keep the car straight.
What's more, things seemed to come up quickly. The stop sign. A
left turn. Another car coming toward us.

Those first few blocks were tough and not nearly as fun as I
had anticipated. The truth was I started to doubt I'd ever be able

to drive a car by myself. My dad seemed to understand what I was feeling because I heard him chuckle softly.

"Now," he said, his voice calm and steady, "I want you to try something for me."

"Okay," I said, unable to hide the shakiness in my voice.

"I want you to aim high."

I made a face. "Aim high?"

"That's right," he said. "When you've been driving, you've been looking only a few feet past the front of the car. I want you to try lifting your eyes and looking further ahead. Don't look right in front of the car."

It took a little practice, but once I got the hang of it, I was able to control the car's steering much more comfortably without the constant adjustments I'd been making earlier. I had plenty of time to brake for stops, and to anticipate changes in the road ahead. Of course, the value of my dad's lesson wasn't confined to driving. More than that, he was teaching me to see the big picture. Well, what was true for my learning to drive is true for investing and retirement as well.

When investing, people too often take the short view. They hear that the stock market is falling, and they panic, thinking they have to react. So they rush to sell. The market changes again. They believe they have to react again. And so it goes. A vicious cycle.

But if you "aim high" and take the longer view, then what may seem like a crisis can be seen in context as a small bump in the road.

I said it before and I'll say it again:

It is all about time IN the market, not TIMING the market.

All of my friends in the financial markets know the wisdom of my dad's driving lesson. So, why do so many of them keep making retirees and soon-to-be retirees crazy?

The financial industry is a multi-trillion-dollar business. Information from analysts, economists, prognosticators, CFAs, CFPs, forecasters, predictors, stock market experts and financial planners jam the broadcast airwaves, pile up email inboxes with electronic newsletters and hurt the backs of postal workers who deliver print editions of personal finance magazines and direct mail. Don't get me wrong. Many of these professionals put the American public first. They are here to inform, educate, and assist you in doing what's best.

But when I come across people who seem to love injecting hysterics into what should be a pretty straightforward process, I look for solid solutions—reliable answers to clear up the pandemonium that is stock market reporting.

But, before I go on, let me be clear.

I believe the stock market is a dynamic institution.
Stocks rise and fall. There is volatility.
But the fact is that, in the long term,
stocks, bonds and real estate are remarkably consistent.

Everyone who has ever saved a dollar knows that even stuffing that dollar in a mattress carries some risk. Inflation. Fire. Theft. This is not hyperbole. It happens—even to the "It can't happen to me" crowd. My point: There are many ways to cut risk. There is a way to ride out market changes and enjoy a satisfying retirement.

I don't have a secret formula. Nor do I have insights that can give individuals an inside track to financial security. If someone promises or guarantees you superior and unusually positive results, you should run. The advice I am giving is rooted in history and common sense—and in your dedication to a steady investing and retirement plan. I am trying to give you a thoughtful, rational perspective on how best to enjoy your retirement after a lifetime of hard work and prudent investing.

There will always be competing opinions available for your digestion. You'll always be able to hear a contrarian opinion. There will always be someone on TV, in your friendship group or in your circle of trusted advisors who will tell you the opposite of what the data says, the opposite of what I am saying, and the opposite of what you feel to be right. What we have is a tool on our side, that, so far, has been remarkably consistent in the long run. That tool is *historical perspective.* If you are a veteran investor who has endured more than one down market without selling all your holdings, or you have a keen sense of historical perspective when it comes to the stock market, go ahead and skip this chapter.

If, however, you feel like many of us, who consider ourselves smart and informed yet we still feel trepidation when it comes to the stock market, then please read on. Read on, because it takes conviction in the benefits of investing in the stock market based on historical data to create the income necessary for you to create the retirement you want. You may well have been invested in the market for your entire working life through 401K plans and the like. You may have told yourself that the market is no place to be in retirement. If that's the case, read on.

Over Time, The Market Goes Up.

In this chapter we will market-proof your mind. As we discussed in Part One in chapters four and five, the media and the financial industry have done a pretty stellar job of scaring Baby Boomers into believing they are in rickety financial shape, and that a stock market dip could mean bad news for your retirement security. You might already have followed the market for long enough that you understand that by its very nature the market contracts and expands, based mostly on investor sentiment. In my experience, even market experts get spooked by dips; it's in *our* human nature to feel fear when we see our precious returns and nest egg drop in value. What we have to remember is this very simple fact: the market has returned an average of ten percent a year for nearly nine decades.

Using data taken from the NYU Stern Business School, which is readily available on their website, you can see the S&P's average annual returns up until 2017, representing 10, 15, 20, 25, 50 and 85 years.[33]

Time Period	*Average Annual Return**
2007-2017 (10 years)	+7.65% per year
2002-2017 (15 years)	+9.29% per year
1997-2017 (20 years)	+6.89% per year
1992-2017 (25 years)	+9.48% per year
1967-2017 (50 years)	+9.98% per year
1932-2017 (85 years)	+10.07% per year

Source: NYU.EDU

It's a common misconception that people who invest in the stock market can lose all their money. You could have lost all your money if you put every penny into a single stock or a single bond, but we are not talking about going for a roulette-based approach to investing. A diversified portfolio of stocks and bonds has never gone to zero. In fact, in the past 50 years, the WORST year for an investor with a portfolio made up of 50 percent stocks and 50 percent bonds was 1974. You would have lost about 12 percent overall for the year. By the way, the same portfolio would have been up 20 percent the following year.

In a number of my blog posts and in my classes, I have spoken at great length about how stocks returned an average of nearly 10 percent from 1900 to 2017, but what about before then?

Now remember, the light bulb wasn't invented until 1879, and the leading cause of death in 1900 was tuberculosis.

So, how did the stock market hold up?

The data from William Bernstein's Efficient Frontier shows that from 1801 to 1900, the stock market returned investors an average of 6.51 percent a year.[34]

At first glance, that appears to be a little disappointing, considering that in the next 100 years, the stock market rose an average of 9.89 percent.

But all is not as straightforward as it seems. You see, in the 1800s, the country saw very little inflation. In fact, something priced at $1 in 1800 cost a little less than a dollar 100 years later, in 1900.

That means that after inflation, stocks from 1800 to 1900 returned 6.76 percent overall. And from 1900 to 2000, after inflation, the stock market's real return was 6.45 percent. You need to subtract out inflation from stock returns to get the real return—the amount of purchasing power your money gained after inflation.

Common Sense Investing is Simple and it Works.

Don't make this more complicated than it is! My investing advice is so simple and straightforward that it is almost a cliché.

It's common sense: invest, diversify and keep a long-term perspective.

It's almost as simple as "buy low, sell high." I don't make any great claims for my advice except that it has worked just fine for more than 100 years. Of course, past performance is no guarantee of future results, but you can't ignore history. You can't ignore it because the trends are so obvious.

In other words, we don't have to recreate the wheel. It works.

Do I really think I know more than all the experts on television and in the financial press?

No, I don't think I know more than they do. Many have degrees in economics, law and finance from prestigious colleges. As I see it, the problem is that, when all smart people accept the same premise, they all logically arrive at the same conclusion. But in this case, the premise is a lie.

The premise: there are people who know what the stock market will do this year. They don't. Not Warren Buffett. Not Alan Greenspan. Not Charles Schwab. Not Jim Cramer. Not *Money* magazine. Not CNBC. Not *The Wall Street Journal*.

But many of the people who preach this stuff actually do believe it.

Most smart people who have been at least a little bit successful are convinced that they have a better understanding of what the markets are going to do than everyone else. They believe that they can time or game the markets and make more money than everyone else. They believe that, by understanding the intricate subtleties of a profit-and-loss statement, they can predict the future. But they can't. I could point to hundreds, if not thousands, of academic papers that have discovered the same thing: no "expert" has *ever* been able to beat the markets consistently.

Have you ever been in traffic on a highway and seen a driver zipping in and out of traffic, shifting lanes, jumping ahead and maybe even driving up the off-ramp lane to get ahead of other cars? And there you are, stuck in your lane, wishing you had the smarts—or the car—to be able to beat the traffic.

But when you get to your exit, you discover that that very same driver is alongside you in the next lane or maybe even behind you.

It may be exciting to drive as if getting ahead of every other car were going to get you to your destination faster, but the simple truth is that slow and steady really does win the race ... and keeps you out of a lot of fender-benders.

Short-term investing. Gaming the system. Beating the odds. It's all the same as   that driver racing ahead two cars, braking hard, cutting in and out of traffic ... only to end up—if he's lucky— exactly where he would have been if he'd just relaxed and stayed in his lane.

The markets are just being the markets. They are not abnormally crazy right now. Nothing out of the ordinary is happening now that hasn't happened for the past 100 years.

The problem is that some people in the media have made it appear as if the market is more crazy than ever before. But that is not true now, just as it hasn't been true before.

Yet because of this barrage of untruth, many viewers believe broadcasters who do not provide historical facts. Viewers worry and struggle based on a poorly-formed hypothesis. Almost everyone who reads these panic-inducing articles will surely come away with heart palpitations.

Boomers view the market with trepidation and fear, saying, "Man, oh man, I'd better be careful. Looks like the market is about to tank. I'd better sell, or buy, or change. I'd better do something and I'd better do it quick."

It is almost never smart to act quickly when it comes to the markets. You should think of the markets and your investments like an ocean liner. If you want to change its direction, you need a lot of time. Time to evaluate. Time to reduce any fast-trigger responses. Turning on a dime is the action of a sprint car in a short race, not an ocean liner designed for the long haul. It is counter-productive to make rash decisions about your retirement investments.

In my opinion, "quick" investing should be called its proper name: gambling. Rolling the dice.

Are you desperate to beat the odds? If you want to win (or lose) big time and in a hurry, you belong at a gaming table in Las Vegas, not preparing for a smart and satisfying retirement.

And If a Crisis Does Hit?

Corrections will always happen. But will a systemic crisis like the Great Depression happen again? At the time of writing this book, the United States has experienced 10 years of record-breaking growth, accounting for half of the world's wealth increase during that time.[35]

Does my "five percent spend" philosophy apply in a down market or during a sustained recession?

Let's break down some of the worst stock market events in the last 10 years. Note what has happened each and every year following a market drop. We used S&P annual returns referenced earlier in the chapter.[33]

97

The Great Recession

- In the 2008 recession, the S&P 500 dropped 36.55 percent.

- In 2009, the S&P went up 25.94 percent.

- In 2010, it rose 14.82 percent.

- In the next three years, it rose 2.10 percent, 15.89 percent and 32.15 percent.

- If you had invested $100 at the beginning of the recession, your nearly $37 loss rebounded by 2013 to around $140.

Dot-com Bubble

- In 2001, the S&P dropped 11.85 percent, and fell 21.97 percent more in 2002.

- It then jumped 28.36 percent in 2003 and 10.74 percent in 2004.

- If you had invested $100 on January 1 2001, by the end of 2004, you'd have a little over $104. If you waited another year, you'd have over $109; and another year later you would have $120.46.

I believe the stock market will *never* hit zero. Sure, it may dip in some places, but it will *always* go back up. The life expectancy of a healthy 65 year-old is around 90. By putting capital into growth investments, such as stocks, you capitalize on a powerful tool that can help you during your retirement years. I'm not promoting that you put all of your money in the stock market, but having a diversified portfolio of stocks and bonds is useful throughout your entire life, including retirement.

My method of taking out five percent still applied *even* through the Great Recession; assuming you stay invested and don't cash out when the market heads south. It's actually a relatively conservative approach; a percentage point or two above generally practiced norms, but certainly not a crazy amount, relative to projected income. For 85 consecutive years, i.e. since the Great Depression, you can spend five percent of your principal and still end up with more money in your retirement than you started with, according to these estimates.

If you retired in 1950 with $100,000 and took out $5,000 a year for next 25 years, you would have ended up with significantly more than $100,000.

If you retired in 1970 with $100,000 and took out $5,000 a year for next 25 years, you would have ended up with significantly more than $100,000.

If you retired in 1990 with $100,000 and took out $5,000 a year for next 25 years, you would have ended up with significantly more than $100,000.

You get my point...

Investments always carry a risk of temporary, short-term losses, but they have always permanently gone up. Of course, past performance does not guarantee future results, but 200 years of American economic history have been incredibly consistent.

Although it is easy to promise that this strategy will always make money, that isn't true. I've noted there is some risk, as the short-term ups and downs of the market mean short-term gains and losses. However, the long-term lesson of the market has been clear: if you take five percent of their investment savings for the rest of their lives, the historical record suggests that they will, more often than not, end with more than you started with. If you spend five percent, in my opinion, you will still have enough for you to enjoy your retirement.

Once people begin to see things with this historical perspective, they start to think that maybe, just maybe, they should be spending some of that hard-earned money. Maybe, just maybe, they should be enjoying some of the money they have saved. The alternative is working when you don't have to, or want to, when you don't actually need to. If you are like the majority of my clients, you have saved your whole life for your retirement. It's time to trust in your planning and to overcome the market fears we hear on from the TV each day.

Some takeaways:

1. The stock market, after inflation, has had a similar average return for more than 200 years.

2. Going forward, while no one can guarantee what will happen, it is important that you base your financial decisions on an incredibly consistent pattern that has persisted for centuries.

3. If you invest in a diversified portfolio of stocks and bonds, you are giving yourself the best chance, statistically, to succeed. Investments such as gold, commodities, certificates of deposit and currencies can have wild and inconsistent returns.

CHAPTER EIGHT:

Your Budget: The Foundation of an Empowered Retirement

We have to assess our potential and limits, envision the final result we desire, make ambitious plans accordingly, and then implement them.
Jimmy Carter

You empower yourself to live an exceptional retirement by creating a solid financial plan. Your plan is based on financial facts, not beliefs or what the media says about the stock market. Your financial reality is yours and yours alone—and any financial news about Boomers not being prepared for retirement does not apply to you. Once you take charge of your financial reality, you know exactly what you have to play with. You'll also be safe in the knowledge that you've allocated resources to those unforeseen circumstances we all can't help but think about. (Remember: this plan covers you for unexpected expenses, which means you should have no limits on living your best retirement!)

I'm going to to walk you through a scenario retirement plan to show you how you can make your own budget. This is common-sense financial planning that I teach to my retirees and soon-to-be-retirees attending my Social Security class. This budget is straightforward, simple and actually pretty easy, *once* you know what you needs to be included.

No surprises, this financial plan includes you spending five percent of your investment income, starting on day one of your retirement. Remember how we said that for the last 200 years there has never been a time except for the Great Depression that spending five percent would leave you in the lurch at some point in your retirement? We're doing it. Right here. We're showing what spending that five percent of your investment income does to your overall monthly income. Start thinking about fulfilling some dreams!

My point in sharing this information with you is that I want you to know that there is no big secret when it comes to retirement budget strategy. I also want you to be empowered with information when you sit down with your advisor (and yes, I *do* still recommend you sit down with your advisor to make sure you maximize your Social Security benefit and diversify your portfolio). There is no magic method here. No widgets and investment guru talk. This information is widely available. The only difference is that I am *getting you to do the work* so that you can enjoy just the right amount of fruit from your retirement tree.

Time and time again people tell me just what a powerful exercise it is to see their plan laid out in front of them on one piece of paper. It's just one sheet of information. Underlying those numbers are years of saving and planning, a smart Social Security strategy and a well diversified investment strategy.

The truth is that all that thought boils down to this one-sheet empowerment tool that shows you:

a) where you are now financially
b) where you will be when a planned change in income happens, and
c) what your financial reality might be if your spouse passes

Seeing those scenarios played out on paper is the ultimate tool for envisioning just how much of an awesome retirement you can have. One of my favorite things about this plan is that nearly everyone who does it is pleasantly surprised at just how much monthly income they have. The true is same for those who don't have "enough" saved for retirement (a minimum of $200K mentioned earlier)—they are nearly always surprised by how much monthly income they have.

Please remember: each individual's circumstances are different. When I sit down with clients, we individualize on a case-by-case basis, taking into account trusts, taxes and everything in between. If you have unanswered questions after completing this exercise, check in with your advisor.

That said, there is no reason to overcomplicate creating your financial plan. Nine cases out of 10 will fit into this simple exercise. The goal of the exercise is to show that a straightforward plan will give you peace of mind and perspective. Let me show you how to figure out how much you need each month, and how much you can prudently use.

These next four steps are the precursor to creating your investment plan. Once we know what we are trying to accomplish, we can get into the nitty gritty of portfolio management.

Before you can move forward with any retirement plan, there are two simple questions you need to answer:

1. How much money do you need each month to live your life?
2. How much money can you safely spend on a monthly basis?

So, here it is: Your clear cut plan to your retirement budget. Let's go.

Step One

First, we need to know your age, your income, assets and debts. And, of course, taxes. Whether you have $200K or $2M saved, it's the same simple process.

a) Your post-retirement income can stem from one or all of the following:
   • Pension payments (note survivor benefits)
   • Social Security payments (this is foundational; read more in Chapter 9)
   • Investment withdrawals
   • Royalties and residues Rental income
   • Part-time income

b) Your assets, such as:
   • Retirement accounts: 401K, IRAs, 403B, deferred-comp
   • Non-retirement savings: Checking CDs, brokerage accounts
   • Real estate: Value of your home, any secondary or rental homes

c) Any outstanding debt:
   • Credit cards Student loans
   • Mortgages from primary, secondary or rental homes

You can input this information into a basic table to help make the information clear:

Income (Part One)

Here is an example of what a post-retirement income might look for an hypothetical couple. The items in this section come from section (a) above.

_____ $1450/MO JANE SOCIAL SECURITY (65)
_____ $775/MO JOHN SPOUSAL (66+10MOS)
_____ $3100/MO JOHN SOCIAL SECURITY (70)
_____ $1400/MO JOHN PENSION (100% survivor benefits to spouse)
_____ $1800/MO JANE PENSION (50% survivor benefits to spouse)

We input the income information into the below table. As you can see we use four columns to signify four scenarios. The first two columns differ thanks to a Social Security strategy. In our example, Jane will claim her Social Security plus a spousal benefit for John until 2022; this plan is represented in column one. Column two show what happens to their income when John reaches the age of 70, at which point he will claim his Social Security. Columns three and four show what income will look like based on Social Security income changes in the event that Jane or John survive each other.

Income Table

	JOHN AGE 66 + 10/MO JANE AGE 65 12/2018	JOHN AGE 70 JANE AGE 68 2/2022	ONLY JANE	ONLY JOHN
INCOME	$1450/MO JANE SS	$1450/MO JANE SS		
INCOME	$775/MO JOHN SPOUSAL	$3100/MO JOHN SS	$3100/MO JOHN SS	$3100/MO JOHN SS
INCOME	$1800/MO JANE PENSION	$1800/MO JANE PENSION	$1800/MO JANE PENSION	$900/MO JANE PENSION
INCOME	$1400/MO JANE PENSION	$1400/MO JOHN PENSION	1400/MO JOHN PENSION	1400/MO JOHN PENSION

Asset and Debt Table

This example of assets and dates represents the information you would get from items b) and c) above.

RETIREMENT	NON-RETIREMENT	REAL ESTATE	DEBT
$220,000 JOHN 401K	$18,000 SAVINGS	$325,000 HOME	$58,000 MORTGAGE
$170,000 JANE 401K		$40,000 R.V.	NO DEBT
$30,000 JOHN ROTH IRA			$4500 CREDIT CARD

Step Two:

Collect together your wills, life and long-term insurance policies. You can also organize your healthcare proxies here, not because they will impact your budget, but because they belong with all these legal documents. We will take into account future sources of funds, such as life insurance policies, or sources of third-part payment for long-term care, when planning your long-term retirement income sources.

Step Three:

It's time to get real about your monthly expenses. Here we will work out exactly how much you need to live each month. You can input your numbers directly onto the expenses worksheet below, or even print my spreadsheet from kennonfinancial.com.

Retirement Expense Worksheet/Budget

Essential Household Expenses

EXPENSE	MONTHLY	ANNUAL
MORTGAGE/RENT		
PROPERTY TAXES		
HOME INSURANCE		
HOA FEES		
ELECTRICITY		
OIL/GAS		
WATER/SEWER		
GARBAGE		
TELEPHONE/CELL PHONE		
CABLE/INTERNET		
POOL SERVICE		
PEST CONTROL		
LAWN SERVICE		
MAINTENANCE/REPAIR		
CARING FOR CHILD/ AGING PARENT		
HOUSECLEANER		
OTHER		

Automotive/Transportation

EXPENSE	MONTHLY	ANNUAL
CAR PAYMENT		
MAINTENANCE/ REPAIRS		
GAS		
LICENSE/ REGISTRATION		
INSURANCE		
OTHER		

Living Expenses

GROCERIES		
EATING OUT		
CLOTHING		
BEAUTY/BARBER		
VACATIONS		
GYM MEMBERSHIP		
NEWSPAPER		
GIFTS		
COUNTRY CLUB		
PETS		
OTHER FUN STUFF		

Medical/ Dental Expenses

Expense	Monthly	Annual
Health Insurance Medicare Premium is $134/mo per person		
Medicare Supplement $0-$200/mo		
Life Insurance		
Other Medical Expenses		
Dental Expenses		
Other		
(Add All Numbers) Total =	/ mo	/ year

We are now ready to take this information and create a spreadsheet that will show us how much money we will have, once we have taken into account our income sources and our expenses.

Step Four (This is the good bit!)

We are ready now to expand on the income information we inputted into our first income table: your investment income row. We work out your investment income by taking the principal amount of your investable assets and deducting 5 percent of that amount by the year. We divided by 12, so that you know how much you can pay yourself per month.

(Keep in mind that while we are basing the monthly income for this row on your principal amount, we will be mostly paying you from interest and dividend payments, assuming your account is up more than 5 percent; therefore you won't necessarily see your principal amount reduce … it *could* actually still increase.)

Before we work out our monthly income by adding together the income streams, let's input our cash savings as our rainy day fund. This covers us for near-term, unexpected expenses. Once we take into account our taxes, we know exactly how much money we can expect each month.

In our example, we see from Step 3 that John and Jane need $4,300 a month to cover their expenses. Once their income, including income from their five percent principal spend, is taken into account, we see that they will have quite a bit more each month.

Column one of the table below shows that John and Jane will receive a gross amount of $7325 a month, or $6425, after tax.

Column two shows that In 2022, when John turns 70 and starts taking his Social Security payments, their monthly pre-tax income will equal $9650, or about $8650, after tax.

Column three shows the income Jane would receive in the event that John were to pass away, and column four shows the income John would receive if Jane were to pass away. Both gross amounts show that the surviving spouse would still have ample funds for day-to-day spending, saving and continuing to enjoy some extra experiences like travel, family or hobbies. All four scenarios show that there will be some extra spending money, relative to their expenses, even when accounting for healthcare expenditure and the like.

Income Table (Part Two - Expanded)

	John Age 66 + 10/mo Jane Age 65 12/2018	John Age 70 Jane Age 68 2/2022	Only Jane	Only John
Income	$1450/mo Jane SS	$1450/mo Jane SS		
Income	$775/mo John Spousal	$3100/mo John SS	$3100/mo John SS	$3100/mo John SS
Income	$1800/mo Jane Pension	$1800/mo Jane Pension	$1800/mo Jane Pension	$900/mo Jane Pension
Income	$1400/mo Jane Pension	$1400/mo John Pension	1400/mo John Pension	1400/mo John Pension
Income	$1400/mo John Pension	$1400/mo John Pension	$1400/mo John Pension	$1400/mo John Pension
Income	$1900/mo Investment Income	$1900/mo Investment Income	$1900/mo Investment Income	$1900/mo Investment Income
Rainy Day	$18,000	$18,000	$18,000	$18,000
Gross	$7325	$9650	$8200	$7300
Taxes	-700	-1000	-1150	-900
Cash	$6425	$8650	$7050	$6400

*PLEASE NOTE- THIS PLAN IS AN EXAMPLE AND DOES NOT REFLECT A REAL-LIFE SCENARIO.

BUDGET NEED: $4300/MO

The great thing about completing this table is knowing that you have a plan in place to cover your expenses. It's such a powerful exercise. We simply figure out where your money is going to come from and when. We inform ourselves with Social Security strategy and are aware of how and when your Social Security income might change. We work out what five percent of your investable assets looks like and add it to your income every year. We take into account taxes and rainy day funds, and voila! You have the basic planning process in place. The next step, of course, is to invest those investable assets into the stock and bond markets under the guidance of your investment advisor, with a diversified plan.

What If I have to Course-Correct?

So what happens if one of those rare "what ifs" tumble from the sky? The reality is *some of us will* experience unexpected expenses (try saying that tongue twister five times over). While you are protected from spending any more than $10,000 a year on medical expenses, you might have a family member you want to help, or a house repair or other expenses you have to deal with.

Now, you will have your rainy day fund set aside so you know that you can cover some expenses. But what if you use it all up?

What happens next depends, of course, on your unique financial circumstances—how much you have saved, how much you have invested and what you need to live on each month.

However, should you find yourself in a position where all of your rainy day money is gone and your living expenses equal your income, you can still course-correct. You can replenish your rainy day fund by reallocating your five percent spend money to your rainy day fund, especially if it feels good to know you have the cash set aside.

Your other option is to consider your invested money as part of your rainy day fund. If you need to, you can divest the money at a later date, and meanwhile the money keeps working for you. If your portfolio is growing as you intend, this makes sense.

If, when you deplete your rainy day funds, the stock market is turbulent, you always have the option to keep some cash in hand.

And if you choose to take a chunk out of your investment portfolio?

The thing to remember is that each financial decision we make has a ramification. If you decide to take an "unscheduled" chunk out of your investment portfolio (an amount that is bigger than your five percent spend allocation), then you get less income from your portfolio each month going forward. It's not that it's a bad idea to cash out some of your portfolio, especially if you need the money—each situation is different. It's just you want to divest and disburse from your portfolio in a judicious manner, and to weigh up the pros and cons before taking action.

At the end of the day, your investment portfolio is your workhorse while you retire. Its gains or losses—and dividends—will be a higher or lower dollar amount depending on how much have invested. Because your dollar return month-by-month, and year- by-year will be reduced as a result of having less invested, you will *permanently* reduce your monthly spend.

Unscheduled portfolio disbursements mean that you will need to reduce the amount you spend in your budget each month. For example, say you have to take out an extra $10,000, the result is that you will receive $40 less per month in income from the investment portfolio. If you take out $100,000, it will permanently reduce your monthly income by $400 a month. You might well be comfortable with that reduction in monthly income, if the rainy day spend is necessary and unavoidable. If the spend is a big splurge, it's worth thinking through how comfortable you are with the decision to take out a big chunk of your investment portfolio.

When tapping more than the five percent of your portfolio, think seriously about it. You have a lot of flexibility in how you spend your retirement investment savings, as long as you fully understand the income impact of spending beyond five percent each year. It's a discussion that happens frequently in my office, and each case takes prudent assessment before a decision is made.

Your Plan is Agile!

Remember this plan is flexible. If you have windfalls or an increase in income for whatever reason, we can amend the budget according to your wants and desires. You'll be able to break your retirement spending plan down to one piece of paper by the time you are done. Stick it on your bathroom mirror and remind yourself that you have a plan. A plan for what could be an amazing retirement!

CHAPTER NINE:

Spend Lest Someone Else Spends For You

Risk comes from not knowing what you are doing.
Warren Buffett

Fresh from the last chapter, you should now have an idea of how much money you have to spend each month, before *and* after you include your five percent spend plan. If you've yet to do the work, or you need some more information,you at least get where your income sources will come from, and hopefully are feeling more optimistic about your financial reality in retirement.

You also come away from the exercise knowing that you have contingency money allocated. With your "rainy day" funds safely stashed away, your living money and extra five percent money are primed for living your best post-work life. There will likely be some tweaks to how and when you access your Social Security and pension savings—because making the right choices for you when it comes to the timing elements of retirement comes down to a strategy that reflects YOUR best plan for your situation. This is an area to consult with your advisor.

In Chapter 8, we reviewed a sample retirement plan that showed us how simple it is to make a retirement budget once we know our expenses, assets and debts, and of course, critically, our income streams.

The first step to being able to work out what those income streams are is to make some decisions about how to access your retirement plans monies and your Social Security payouts. We brought up some questions about pension plans and Social Security; these raise additional questions about Social Security and retirement spending strategies, all before you can make your final decision about when to start taking payouts from your Social Security, or whether to take an annuity or a lump sum payment from your 401K, for example.

In this chapter we will dig a little deeper into some of the underlying spending requirements of your budget, so that you know the reasoning behind those variable Social Security numbers, and age-related changes in income.

While your financial reality has very little to do with the government stats we see in the media, the one place the government's calculations do factor into your life is *when you are required to spend your money.*

Yes indeed, you are required by the government to spend some of those pre-tax retirement savings, and you do have deadlines!

What happens when you don't spend some of your money? Penalty taxes. Avoidable, unnecessary penalty taxes. And none of us want to lose what could be a bright and bold retirement to a bunch of taxes that don't need to happen.

If you don't spend some of your money, Uncle Sam will.

By now we understand Spendophobia, the relative reliability of the stock market over time, and the power of creating retirement security by investing in a diversified portfolio of stocks and bonds.

If this information is not enough to empower you to spend your cash, I hope that knowing that the government will spend your money if you don't is enough to you to give yourself a (smart) spending license.

Knowing what your *spending requirements* are is emboldening. Sure, the government sets spending requirements because it wants its tax revenue from all that pre-tax money you saved over the last 20-40 years. Let's face it, Uncle Sam didn't set spending requirements because there is a government mission to help you live large in retirement (although, on a side note, they'd sure look good if Boomers did start spending more thanks to the jobs and prosperity you would be creating).

The excellent side-benefit to *having* to withdraw the money is that it makes those of us who are "spend shy" a bit more "spend authorized." That said, many people withdraw their RMD with no intention of spending; they place the distributions in the bank. While many people resent the RMD requirements because they don't want to have to take out the money, it is a reality we can work in your favor. Hopefully by now you are feeling "spend smart" and if you are not now, I sure hope to get you there by the end of Part Three.

So, let's go ahead and talk about the two main considerations you need to make when understanding your retirement income: the Required Minimum Distribution rule, and your Social Security strategy.

Required Minimum Distribution (RMD):

When we reach 70 and one-half years of age, the government *requires* us to begin withdrawing from our pre-tax retirement accounts. The requirement to withdraw from your retirement account is called a Required Minimum Distribution (RMD). The government sets a required minimum distribution (RMD) age because it wants to tax you on the distributions from all that retirement money you saved pre-tax.

The RMD rule applies to *almost* every kind of retirement plan. It covers employer-sponsored plans, including profit-sharing, 401(k), 403(b), and 457(b) plans. Traditional IRAs and IRA-based plans such as SEPs, SARSEPs, and SIMPLE IRAs also fit into the RMD rule.

There are two exceptions to the RMD rule: your Roth IRA which you never have to withdraw from—though I can't imagine why you would not, as you have already paid tax on that Roth income. The second exception is your 401k, if you continue to work past age 70.5, in which case you do not have RMDs until you retire.

The age you are *required* to begin withdrawals is arbitrary in terms of *your* personal retirement plan; it has nothing to do with when would be a good time for you to spend. (In case you forgot, day one is a good day to start on your smart spending plan!) If you so choose, you can start spending your RMD, or more, at age 59 and one-half. It's all about what's right for you.

As you age, the RMD increases. At age 75, you are required to disburse 4.37 percent and at 80, 5.35 percent. The government is of course making sure you pay tax on that income during your lifetime. No fear. You'll already be on top of that whole RMD thing.

You may incur some more living expenses as you grow into your 80s and 90s; medical bills will be capped, but you might have assisted living expenses to consider. At the same time, you may be spending less on travel and the pricier experiences of earlier retirement.

So, wouldn't it be nice to know that by taking charge of your spending, you are replacing potential penalties with spending on the things that matter to you.

That's what the Retirement Revolution is all about: taking charge of your spending so that you spend according to YOUR life plan. Not the government's, and not any other arbitrary expectation or requirement. It's all about spending in line with your design for life.

Let's take a look at what the RMD looks like in practice:

Imagine you have $100K in your retirement plan.
Based on the requirement to spend 3.65 percent, you are required to withdraw $3,650 of that amount in the year you turn 70 and one-half.

Three important points to remember:

1. You don't have to take the money from the principal. If your IRA earned the equivalent of 3.65 percent in income, dispersing that amount is sufficient.

2. If you have multiple IRAs, you can lump the amounts together and withdraw the 3.65 percent of all of the accounts from one account.

3. The 3.65 percent requirement was correct at the time of publishing in 2018. Check for updates to the RMD each year on the IRS website, or ask your advisor.

And an **even more important** point to remember:

If you don't withdraw that 3.65 percent, the government will fine you HALF of the amount you should have withdrawn. (You read that right: FIFTY percent of the amount you should have withdrawn; or, put another way, 1.83 percent each year.)

In the $100K example I gave, that equals an avoidable donation to Uncle Sam of $1,582 EACH YEAR.

Imagine you have $500K or even $1M in savings, and do the math. You certainly don't want to lose an unnecessary 1.83 percent of your savings each year. (That's a little over $18,000 a year if you have a million in the bank!)

If you do not spend at least the amount the RMD requires, you are essentially throwing money away. You'd be surprised how many people don't pay attention to the RMD, until the IRS lets them know. If you have a financial advisor, I can't imagine a world in which they would not make sure you spent at least your RMD!

No one wants to pay a fine on their unspent savings.

Picture this scenario: you have a great year of returns on your portfolio, only to find that you didn't spend the 3.65 percent you should have. You lose an even bigger chunk, thanks to all those gains you made. If the market goes down, you didn't just miss out on enjoying some of your gains, you lost an even bigger chunk to your RMD penalty.

So it's pretty important that you do spend your money, because if you don't, the government will spend it for you—and not on the cruise you always dreamed of, or sending your grandkids to that incredible STEM camp next summer.

It's OK to start spending the money you are making in your retirement accounts. You don't have to limit yourself to 3.65 percent, you can spend more. And you don't have to wait until 70.5. You can start spending on day one of retirement.

How to Make Sure You Don't Get Hit by the RMD

As far as my philosophy goes, you never have to worry about requirement minimum distributions. Why? Because when you spend five percent of your investment income, including some of your principal in the event of a down market (keep that historical perspective engaged!), you are already meeting the Required Minimum Distribution rule.

You'll need to increase your spending slightly at 80, and again at 85, and again at 90, but you will be pro at living your empowered retirement at that point, so increasing your spending won't be hard once you get going.

And remember, I am suggesting that you start spending five percent on the day you retire. On day one of reaching 66, or whatever age you choose to retire, your retirement plan goes into effect. And that retirement plan includes you spending five percent of your income a year … until you reach 75, when your spend is going up to 5.35 percent based on the RMD, not on any advice from me or any other advisor.

You can start spending at 66 because your money is working for you in a diversified account. You don't work any more, but your stock portfolio does. You DO still have income, assuming you are set up in a adequately diversified portfolio of stocks and bonds with at least half of the money in stocks.

Social Security

Getting your Social Security strategy right is *foundational* to your retirement. For many people it is their sole source of income. For the bulk of Boomers, it is a critical component of their income. Therefore we need to make sure you get the most out of your Social Security because it is an important string on your income bow.

I want you to take this information in before you go to the Social Security office. Unfortunately, the Social Security office does a poor job helping people strategize to maximize their benefits. Really, it is not their job. Their job is get you in and out as quickly as possible. Arm yourself with some key strategies and rules you need to get the most your of your Social Security. You've paid into the system for years; let's get you what you have earned.

And remember, we are making you a real retirement plan, not just so you have a base income to live from. We are doing this foundational financial work so that you are in a position to live your BEST retirement. This is one of your most important seeds to sow.

See that pile of money on the table?
That's yours. There is more than you know. Don't leave it.

There are myriad Social Security strategies for married couples. Whether you are married or not, there are lots of ways to get the most out of your Social Security benefit. Choosing the right strategy for you can maximize your benefit as much as $100,000 over your lifetime, so it's important to get it right.[36]

Whether your choices make you as much as $100K, or just a few thousand extra, taking the time to know your best Social

Security path is worthwhile. Getting Social Security right is not as simple as many make it out to be. Setting up the right strategy for you comes down to more than picking an age to start claiming your benefit.

When it comes to Social Security, there are many rules to be taken into consideration. That's why I started giving Social Security classes from my office in Sarasota. My class is no sales pitch. Everyone is welcome, and I see this knowledge- share as me paying my good fortune forward to my community.

If there's one thing I love about doing my Social Security classes, it's seeing the empowerment on my students' faces. They realize that they are in a much better position than before they walked in the door. No money left on the table for these folks. They also are one step closer to taking charge of their *whole* retirement picture.

Once you have your Social Security strategy in place, you are in a much more empowered position to start making some *real* retirement plans based on your income. And by real, I mean making-retirement-dreams-happen real. But first, back to the nuts and bolts of a solid financial foundation from which to hatch those dreams.

Once you get your Social Security strategy in place, you will know:

a. How much money you have to live on each month (before you consider your IRA investment income).

b. What your monthly income will be if you outlive your spouse (this information is good to have in your back pocket).

There are a countless scenarios for every retiring individual and couple in the USA today. The example above goes to show just how much extra benefit you can give yourself, once you know the lingo to include on your Social Security application.

To pick the right one for you, you are better off consulting with your financial advisor, assuming they know their Social Security rules, rather than visiting your local Social Security office.

As well as strategies, there are also countless rules, which again are best navigated with a professional. That said, I'm going to lay out a few key Social Security strategies that work within the rules, because if you can avoid tripping on these, you are in a good starting position. There are some core pieces of knowledge that will pay you handsomely. I'm going to share them with you.

Social Security Strategy #1: The Restricted Spousal Benefit

The Restricted Spousal benefit is the most important Social Security strategy for married couples. It's important to note that this strategy currently only applies to those of us born in 1953 or earlier, and you have to wait until you are age 66 to apply. Also remember, it only works if your spouse has *already* applied for Social Security.

The "restricted application" allows you to collect half of your spouse's Social Security while your own continues to grow. Your spouse continues to claim their full benefit at the same time.

It is an incredibly powerful benefit that gives you what I like to call "free money from age 66 to 70." At 70, you then change over to your own benefit, which has been maximized by deferring. I call it "free money" because that is exactly what it is. If you were going to wait until 70 anyway, and you didn't know about this strategy, you would have missed out on an additional income—half of what your spouse was receiving. That's four years of not receiving an additional half of your spouse's income each month.

If one of you has a significantly larger benefit than the other, the person with the largest amount should defer Social Security for as long as possible. The longest you can defer to is age 70. Social security, on average, grows eight percent each year you don't withdraw your benefit. You obviously want the person with the larger amount to gain eight percent each year. Over four years, that is 32 percent growth.

Deferring the larger social security income check is a no-brainer, assuming you can afford to delay the income until age 70. You can collect half of your spouse's income if that amount is worth more than *all* of your income. To clarify: the most you can get is half of your spouse's income as it stood at retirement age, i.e. at age 66. You don't get to claim half of what their income would be at age 70.

Take the real-world example below. What you are seeing here is my mom and dad's Social Security strategy (shared with their permission, of course):

The starting scenario:
- My mom and dad retire at age 66.
- My dad is eligible for $2,400 a month. My mom is eligible for $1,000 a month.

The strategy:
- My dad was able to apply for a "restricted spousal application."
- This allowed him to trade his $2,400 a month for half of my mom's Social Security payment: $500 a month.
- Meanwhile my dad's benefit continues to grow at eight percent a year.
- He will revert to his benefit at age 70.
- If my dad predeceases my mom, my mom will get my dad's benefit, which has been maximized.

The outcome:
- My folks live off $1,500 a month until age 70.

(My mom's benefit of $1,000 and my dad's spousal benefit of $500) At age 70, my dad's Social Security payment will be $3,360 a month. If my mom outlives my dad, she will get his spousal benefit of $3,360.

A Note About Survivor Benefits & Divorce

Besides the fact that this strategy will likely give you more Social Security income during your lifetime, you are also protecting your spouse. Remember, the surviving spouse will receive the biggest of your two Social Security checks.

Survivor benefits mean that if the spouse with the smaller benefit outlives the spouse with the larger benefit, the surviving spouse will receive the larger benefit. It's good to know that you can apply for Survivor Benefits at age 60, two years earlier than you can claim regular Social Security. You can continue to claim your Survivor Benefit until age 70.

Divorced? You still have the same Restricted Spousal Benefit and Survivor Benefit rights, as long as you were married for 10 years or more, and you are not remarried. If your ex-spouse passes away, you are eligible for all of his or her Social Security check, assuming it is more than yours.

Social Security Strategy #2: Timing is Everything

One thing is for sure. If you can delay claiming your Social Security benefit until age 70, you will get more from it. One way people delay Social Security is to continue working until age 70. Assuming you love your work, this is a great idea. If you are in a position to hold off claiming your Social Security benefit until age 70, and you expect to live a long retirement, it makes sense to benefit from that average of eight percent annual growth we talked about in the first Social Security strategy. (And keep in mind that eight percent growth applies to both married and non-married people; it's definitely for everybody.) The earliest you can take your

Social Security is 62, and the latest you can start taking your benefit is 70. When you decide to start taking Social Security income is down to your personal situation: your health, how long you expect to live, and whether or not you depend on that income to live. If you can stretch it out, stretch it as far as you can.

Another benefit to delaying your Social Security payments until age 70 is that you better protect yourself against inflation, because the larger benefit that you will be entitled to receive will also get larger "raises" when the Social Security system approves cost of living adjustments. (The government makes an annual cost-of-living adjustment to Social Security according to the Consumer Price Index, purely to protect you from inflation.)

But wait, don't you get more checks if you cash out at age 62? Does it not make sense to take those extra checks? Well, honestly, this all comes down to how long you live. Age 80 is the magic age. If you think you will live longer than age 80, go ahead and DELAY. Some of us are going to live past 100. Once you start taking your Social Security benefit, it's set. You want that larger check. If you don't think you'll live past 80, let's get real and start getting those checks at age 62! It's your call at the end of the day.

Social Security Strategy #3:
Work & Social Security Don't Mix Well

It's true, you can work and collect Social Security at the same time. But you have to be smart about working within the rules, or it can *cost* you to work. You can make up to $17,040 in 2018 (check SSA.gov for updated amounts each year).

If you collect Social Security before your Full Retirement Age (age 66 for people born between 1943 and 1954) and make more than $17,040, you will be charged $1 for every $2 you go over. The IRS only cares about earned income; they don't care about income from your investment accounts. They also only look at the income from the person who is collecting benefits. They do not look at any income your spouse may be receiving.

Once you are at full retirement age, which is age 66, assuming you were born before 1955, you can earn as much as you like and still claim your Social Security benefit.

Consider this example:

- Ms. Nurse is 62 and is earning $50K a year.

- She also claims her Social Security benefit of $1,500 a month ($18,000 a year)

- $33K of her $50K salary is over the limit of $17,040

- She will be penalized a dollar for every two dollars she makes over the limit. In this case, her penalty is $16,500 a year.

- She would therefore only make around $1,500 in Social Security benefits.

- The moral of the story?

- Be careful when taking Social Security before retirement age!

You still likely have a ton of questions concerning Social Security. The most often asked question in my class? You guessed it...

Question #1: Is Social Security going to be around for my whole retirement?

For your generation, yes. Your Social Security is intact. And I am telling you this based on the facts, not on rhetoric, and not on anything you heard on the radio. Your Social Security is not going to go bankrupt in your lifetime.

All the academics say the same thing: the system is not going to become insolvent. When you review the Trustees Report, the system is not in as bad shape as we think.

Social Security is fully funded until 2034. By then, the SSA does state that the law governing benefit amounts may change, because current payroll taxes will only pay about 77 cents of each dollar of scheduled benefit. Many Boomers will be retired in 2034, but they are not going to be affected. There are several proactive strategies already being implemented in order to make up for any shortfalls in funding.

Any changes in Social Security benefit will not affect those of us 55 or older. In fact, the Boston College Center for Retirement Research is quoted as stating, *"Don't start benefits early because Social Security has money problems… you won't get more if you do. Nearly all proposals to fix Social Security would also protect those aged 55 and older."*

Question #2: Taxes? What the heck is provisional income and how does it affect my taxes? (And haven't I already paid them?!)

You're right: Social Security didn't used to be taxed. It is now, for many of us. Ronald Reagan's administration started charging tax for Social Security withdrawals in 1983. The government figures you paid into your Social Security payments, pre-tax, kind of like a guaranteed IRA. Not everyone is going to pay tax on their Social Security benefits. To work out whether or not YOU will pay tax, you need to determine your *provisional income.*

How to work out your provisional income:

½ of your Social Security

+ traditional pension payments

+ retirement account withdrawals

+ plus earned income (if still working)

+ interest from CD's, dividends from stocks, interest from bonds

= Your provisional income

If your provisional income exceeds certain limits, you must pay federal income tax on your Social Security (at whatever your overall tax rate is). For married couples, the limit is $44,000, and for single filers the limit is $34,000.

My intention in this chapter was to highlight that there are important strategic moves to make when it comes to (a) dispersing money from your investment accounts and (b) making the right timing, work, and spousal benefit choices when it comes to Social Security. The choices you make at the beginning of your retirement will impact the decades of income you receive for the rest of your life.

Your three key takeaways:

1. Spend five percent a year of your savings from day one of your retirement to make sure YOU are the one who gets the money you've saved, and not the government. RMD's don't matter to you because you are already empowered to spend your hard-working savings.

2. Social Security is 100 percent funded for your generation, and there is a lot of money on the table that gets missed every year. It's not just a matter of going to the Social Security office and applying. You need to know the rules before you walk in, so that you can make the most beneficial timing and spousal benefit strategy for you.

3. You own your retirement. By knowing the Social Security strategies, you are giving yourself an incredible foundation to a) know how much money you have to live and play with, and b) really drill down on what kind of life you want to live now that you are in the new era of freedom. What does your most fulfilled retirement look like to you?

Chapter Ten:

The Inheritance Myth, Revisited

It's best to give while your hand is still warm.
Philip Roth

When you think about setting up your heirs with an inheritance, what do you want to accomplish? Perhaps you want your kids and their kids to have a financial security blanket, or perhaps you want them to be able to afford experiences that you couldn't. Perhaps your kids need the money.

Perhaps the idea of inheritance is ingrained in you, as it is many of us. It's just what we do. Thousands of years of human history across cultures indicate that we humans like to pass forward our wealth to our offspring—passing the farm down the kids, chiefs passing their roles to their first-borns ... the Mongols gave the parents' tent to youngest born, who typically cared for them.

The expectations of passing down your material wealth to your children have been perpetuated for thousands of years; it's no wonder that you're inclined to believe that it's something that we do.

For sure, inheritance is a lasting gift you can pass forward to your family or loved one, to make sure that they have security they might not otherwise have.

We know that the generations that follow the Boomers are not as well prepared for retirement, often because they have different pressures than the Boomer generation (more expensive healthcare, less job security and large student loans).

For those of us in a position to pass wealth down through inheritance, it's a good feeling.

But, here's the thing: If there's one dismaying aspect of working with families and their money, it's seeing the discomfort and disharmony that can arise with inheritance. What should be a beautiful thing—paying forward a financial gift that will provide security and perhaps opportunity to your loved ones—often ends up causing legal issues, anger and resentment.

Am I against inheritance? No, not at all. But I will say this: I've seen too many inheritance wastes and fights in my time. As a result, I counsel my clients to first use their money for their own enjoyment, and if they do want to use it to help their children they should do it while they're still here. You have an opportunity to model how you want your children to steward your hard-earned money. You also have an opportunity to see first-hand your money being put to good use—frankly, good use that you get to dictate. It is, after all, your money.

Of course, many of us still plan to provide an inheritance; in which case, it is critical we express our wishes very clearly in a will during the estate planning process. Writing a will is obviously elementary advice, but it's still important to mention. Only 44 percent of Americans have a will.[36] For those folks that don't have the will, the State decides what happens to the money, and usually that means the money goes forward to the surviving spouse or kids in a lump sum.

But even with wills stipulating who gets what, and when and how they get it through a trust, inheritances can still lead to family feuds and will contests. It's not always the case, but money gets messy when its fate isn't written down with words as clearly as it is represented in numbers on the page.

I could write an entire book devoted to inheritance stories. Instead I will give three vignettes that highlight my points about the challenges of inheritance. I think it is safe to say that we've all heard stories of wasted inheritances, family feuds, and even inheritances getting locked up due to lack of proper estate planning.

You can take the cautionary tales that follow with a grain of salt. Your kids might be financially responsible and connect to the sanctity of the financial gift you may plan to bestow upon them. They may thoroughly respect YOUR lifetime of earning, saving and prudently investing this money, possibly by making sacrifices along the way. For some, knowing the story behind your money may be enough for them to inherit the funds and to put them to responsible use.

Again, I've seen enough scenarios play out where, because the money isn't earned by the heirs, they lose a sense of its value. Think about how you might spend a windfall relative to a paycheck. An inheritance is the ultimate unearned bonus. That's not to say you shouldn't give an inheritance at all. After these stories, we'll talk about the smart way to give while living.

The Case of the Derailing Inheritance

The couple in this story had three children. Two of their children were successful. They had completed college, had found good jobs and had made their parents proud. The third child was something of a black sheep. His struggles began in his teen years, starting with trouble at school, and drinking and using drugs while still a teenager. Even into young adulthood he had not "found his way" and he didn't have a real job or direction. Still, the family worked hard to keep him part of their family unit.

The couple loved their family and had saved a considerable amount with the intent to leave it to their children. Tragically, the couple passed away at a relatively young age. First the father, of a heart attack, and then the mother, of ovarian cancer.

Just as they'd planned, they had left a significant inheritance to their children. Each of these children—two of which were already comfortable in their own right—now found themselves very wealthy.

What happened next was almost a cliché. The two children who were "well adjusted" and doing well suddenly seemed to fall apart. Their earlier career goals fell by the wayside, unnecessary after they received their inheritance.

With so much money and free time, and with no one to guide them, they were left to make their own choices. At every opportunity, they seemed to make the wrong one. They started in with the "wrong crowd"—people who knew how to take advantage of others with some disposable money. They partied. They bought cars and other high- priced things they didn't need. They both began to struggle with substance abuse. It should come as no surprise that they made foolish investments.

Despite being the "well adjusted" children, they were simply unprepared for the opportunities and responsibilities that came with having so much money so quickly. Although they were thrilled with their "windfall" when they first got it, it didn't take long for their money to fail to give them any lasting joy or peace.

They kept spending more and seeing less of a "return." It wasn't long before their bad choices ended up losing them their money. Those two "responsible" children had lost just about everything.

Ironically, it was the third child, the black sheep, who worked hard to keep it together and did everything he could to help his siblings. However, it is a very sad story—a morality tale of sorts. A perfect illustration of the fallacy that inheritance is always a wonderful thing. Sometimes—too often—inheritance is a burden that weighs down its recipient.

The Case of the Ruinous Promise

Christine and Jeremy are quite wealthy. They have about $10 million in assets, and they're in their 60s. Knowing they wouldn't spend all their money, they set up a trust. They invited in their three children so that everyone knew what was going on, and so they would have a relationship with the attorney.

The children had no idea just how wealthy their parents actually were, until that meeting. Christine described how this promise of future money changed them, evenbefore they could have it in their hands. From that day forward, the kids were much less motivated to work. Gary, the eldest, had been going on for weeks about being promoted to head editor of the newspaper company he worked for, but when their son met with them for brunch, he said, "I don't need to go up any higher. I like it where I am."

Allyson, the middle child, had been adamant about working in her bakery, but she was considering hiring a second manager to take on some of her responsibilities. She didn't think she'd need as many hours.

Jeff had even brought up to his parents the idea of him going back to school to try and get a second bachelor's degree. This plan of his involved taking some time off from his construction job in order to focus on his studies.

Christine and Jeremy found themselves in a predicament. The money that was eventually headed their way had already turned their hardworking children into a trio of lazy, entitled kids.

"Now we're trying to figure out how to break the news to our kids that they're not going to get anything," Jeremy said. He folded his hands in his lap. "It's not like we want to leave them with nothing, but what good will it do for them to think that they can slack off and expect to get paid for it?"

The next day, they returned to their attorney and with heavy hearts, told him to change their plan. They were going to give their money to the American Heart Association, the Cystic Fibrosis Foundation and other disease-awareness groups.

Their children were furious.

The family still talks, but there's a somewhat petty tension at family get-togethers. It's become an unspoken rule not to talk about inheritance, or money at all.

The Case of Two Daughters

Two daughters split an inheritance of $1 million in a lump sum. One of those daughters, Tammy, worked with an advisor to roll the money over in a tax-efficient manner. She was able to get the money working for her in a long-term plan that would allow her to properly use the money throughout her life. The second daughter, Carol, to whom she had always been close, then dropped the news that she was engaged to a guy named Adam. They happily lived in Las Vegas, but her fiancé had a gambling problem.

Six months later, Tammy came into her advisor's office one morning with her lips pressed in a tight scowl, her fingers tapping impatiently on her arm. "Carol blew it," she said.

Not only did Carol and Adam take all $500,000 at once (which is a huge tax-time bomb), but they gambled it all away within six months. Tammy found out after a desperate call from Carol to borrow some of her money to meet the house payment for the month.

"Half a million dollars, up in smoke!" she cried, throwing her arms up in the air.

Blame was tossed left and right. The minutes on their phone bills were skyrocketing, but each minute was spent arguing. Now, they don't even waste their time; Carol refuses to believe that spending away her money was wrong, and Tammy is too tired of arguing at a brick wall. Although their mother had faith in her daughters that everything would be fine, this inheritance essentially split her family in half. When they were little, Tammy and Carol used to stay up for hours at night, telling each other stories when they were supposed to be going to bed. They haven't spoken to each other in three years.

Giving While Living

The three stories above show how an inheritance can be more of a burden than a blessing. Yes, there are many stories and times when children steward their inheritance successfully. Those examples are usually the result of parents using money wisely in their children's lives and teaching them to be wise stewards of money.

But too often, they don't.

How much better it would be if parents who view their investments as a "someday" inheritance for their children used that money wisely with their children while they were still alive—getting the enjoyment of sharing the fruits of their labor with their hopefully appreciative children. I also have seen the joy, connection and help that results from helping family in real time—on your terms, when the need is most, or the benefit is optimal.

There's a better, more intentioned way to pay at least some of your bequest forward. A way that keeps you in charge.

Three rules for providing an inheritance during your lifetime:

This set of rules is about you taking care of you first. You've worked hard, and saved diligently for your whole life. You've earned a fulfilling retirement, and you need to be provisioned for your own rainy day needs. You are in charge of how your money is spent. You might have charitable goals you want to meet, in addition to taking care of your family.

As you follow these rules, do so with positive regard for your retirement goals and intentions. If you want to splurge on yourself, you can. You don't have to leave anything behind. If you do want to give to your family, make sure you have these three golden rules in place:

- First, you take care of yourself. Have your budget in place, and your investments set to work.

- Gift only from your five percent spending money, and only if you can afford it.

- If you have less than $250,000 in your savings, keep that money working for you; don't pay that forward yet, lest you need it.

Smart Ways to Pay Cash and Assets Forward.

My message about giving to your kids and grandkids while you are able to see the joy it brings is really about enhancing life and deepening connections. But if you have significant assets and you want to pay some of those funds forward, there are a couple of ways to do this more efficiently than providing an inheritance. Always check these methods with your advisor and accountant before putting them to work.

- The IRS allows you to give cash gifts to your children each year, tax-free. Currently (2018) the limit is $15,000 per year ($30,000 for a married couple).[37]

- You can make the choice to give cash gifts year to year, or when you consider it advantageous to your children— for example, when they are buying a house or paying off student debt.

- Give stock rather than cash—especially if they pay at a lower tax rate.

The Real Inheritance: Connection.

Inheritance is often thought of as the final gift, but when you take charge of your giving during your retirement, inheritance becomes a lasting gift with much more meaning. It is your opportunity to use your resources to enhance your connection with your loved ones, to create memories and create a living legacy that remains in the hearts of your children. Now, of course, you don't have to give a thing in order to have a strong connection with your children or grandchildren. But if you want to support your kids, doing so when you are here is the best way forward.

Want to help your child or grandchild buy a house? Go for it. Do it. Now.

Want to help your grandkid take riding lessons? Awesome. Make it so—stat! Pay for those riding lessons and watch her ride as much as possible. That way, you will enjoy your gift to her as much as she enjoys it. And, even better, she will always associate the happiness and accomplishment of riding with you.

Does your grandchild have special educational needs? You can lift them up, and see them thrive thanks to your gifts.

The beauty of giving to your kids while you are here is that you are able to see how your gift enhances their lives. You're still in the picture and able to watch their faces light up when they find out that they're suddenly able to do a little more with your help.

You get to watch small bits of your legacy in action: Maybe you're able to laugh at the glob of paint that splatters on your daughter's apron as she paints her office because you bought the paint. You can push on your grandson's back as he learns to ride the new bike you bought him. You're still able to rally up a storm on Black Friday because damn it, you're going to get your hands on this 82" TV so that you can watch your son *cry* on Christmas morning (and your son *never* cries).

Your granddaughter may want to take piano lessons *and* karate, but your son can only afford one or the other. If you were able to give your son a little financial help every month, you could fund one of your granddaughter's passions. You might have to come to her karate championship still dressed in the formal attire of her piano recital, but wouldn't it be worth it to see your granddaughter's glowing grin as she holds up her golden trophy? You helped put it in her hands.

Your son could have been struggling to open up his art supply store for years. Instead of waiting until you pass on to give him the cash to overspend on this store, you can send him little financial boosts each month until his store is up on its feet. You can go to the grand opening party and watch your son put up the welcome sign for the first time. You get to experience your gift at work.

> *A living inheritance is an opportunity*
> *to create harmony and strengthen bonds.*

Money and passing on are two of the most difficult things to talk about for many of us. For some families, the expectation of inheritance is such a given that it can be a shock, and dare I say it, a hurtful shock, when a child does not inherit from their parent.

It's important to have honest conversations about money with your loved ones. For example, if you are planning to give to them during your lifetime, it helps to let your family members fully understand your plan. You naturally need to keep your boundaries and privacy, as you see fit. Remember our vignette in this chapter that showed the damage revealing your wealth can do. Having an honest conversation with your kids about inheritance is in some ways a gift because it might help them plan for their future. For example, the children of the Gates and Warrens, two of the wealthiest couples in the world, know they will not inherit their parents' wealth. The money is going to the Gates Foundation. The children should plan accordingly.

It comes down to your individual relationship with your children as how open you want to be about your wealth, and what will be passed on or not passed on. You know your children, and you know what is right for you.

A Theoretical Positive Inheritance Story (they DO happen!).

One retired Boomer, Susan, whom we will meet again in Part Three, has a great handle on paying her gifts forward. Her husband passed away some 15 years ago. A couple of years after retirement, she decided to sell her home and buy a smaller place. She had the ability to give some of the proceeds of her home sale to her children to help them with their student debt, mortgages and a grandchild's medical bills. This money came at a time when the kids could really use it. Susan had ample retirement savings and was not burdened by the gift she made. Sure, she could have splurged, but she wanted to help her kids. Susan's parents had passed when she was young, and she had been supported by nuns who helped her get through college and even a Masters degree. She knew the value of meaningful financial support, and felt a great deal of satisfaction to see how her help during her lifetime eased her children's burdens.

Susan has told her kids that there will not be any inheritance upon her passing. She has plenty to live on and intends to spend her savings. Her kids appreciate the gifts she has already given, and continue to thank her for the difference it made to their ability to start businesses and to save for their own children's education. Susan had full control over how her money was spent, and lives knowing that her money was put to good use and benefitted her whole family. No penny was squandered.

Your three main takeaways when it comes to inheritance:

- Take care of yourself first. Stick to your budget and spending plan.
- Give with intention, forethought and connection: When there is most need or for the most optimal benefit.
- You don't *have* to bequeath anything to anyone, but please have a will in place!

So when it comes to inheritance, you have many opportunities to take charge of how you pay your money forward, if that's what you want to do.

As with all aspects of retirement planning, if you want to provide an inheritance to a loved one or multiple family members, factor your willingness to give during your retirement into your retirement values and your spending budget. And plan. Plan well.

PART THREE

CHAPTER ELEVEN:

Retirement 2.0

Retirement is the ugliest word in the language.
Ernest Hemingway

The truth is that a REAL retirement plan is one that is based on what brings you joy, meaning and personal success. Our expectations of retirement have expanded since your parents' retirement. Boomers saw an unprecedented accumulation of wealth in their working lives, and they have redefined expectations of retirement. Whatever your dream retirement looks like, each of us should be able to expect this from our post-work life chapters: A fulfilling, empowered, spectacular retirement.

Now, Part Two was intended to be all about the nuts and bolts of a sound retirement plan: How to create a real retirement budget, to show you what that five percent spend money looks like, to explain how required minimum distributions and Social Security impact your requirement to spend. We also showed some of the smart ways you can pay money forward to your kids, or causes you care about. Financial planning is a required activity in order to be prepared for a financially secure retirement, unless you want to end up overspent or, more realistically, underspent.

> *All the financial planning in the world does*
> *not necessarily precede a happy retirement.*

Once you know what you want from retirement (hint: it's about more than money), *and* know how much money you have (we can't get around that), you are ready to make a real plan. You are now ready to make a plan that is about you, your values and your aspirations—not the average person in a government stat, or based on a news program or other fear-based resource. Once you know what you want, tell your advisor, or if you are your own advisor, set your goals accordingly.

If there is one upside to our digitally interconnected world, it is the increase in dialogue we are having about rethinking retirement. What comes to mind when you think of the traditional retirement? If you are like many of the people I speak with, the general gist of modern day retirement looks like this: Work 40 years, then stop for a life of long days playing golf or bridge with friends. We've been sold this view by, well, society, but it's capitalized upon by the media and the investment industry. And we are reading plenty about those retirement choices online and in books. We are also reading about the alternative road: the people who are on that road I like to call members of the 5 Percent Club!

A traditional retirement of leisure and "good livin'" is the quintessential image of the middle and upper middle class retirement in American culture. Sure, we see commercials with retirees sharing active time with their grandkids and seeing the world, too. It's all part of the grand cliché. Modern day retirement is based on the myth that has been sold to us.

I believe we have been sold short when it comes to retirement.

For a start, for the many folks who don't have enough funds saved for a golf-in- the-sun style retirement, it does not reflect a reality. It serves to enhance a feeling that we are missing out, and I don't think I'm alone in saying we don't need any more of that in the modern era. For those of us who have the funds available, it's a design for life that doesn't necessarily ring true with us at all—not if that's *all* there is to retirement. The image also assumes that your value as a person in society is summed up by leisure pursuits. None of us suddenly become fallow because we don't have to officially work for a paycheck anymore. The idea that retirement is all leisure and no contribution is short-changing our imaginations.

We Need a New word for Retirement.

As Jimmy Carter said in his book, *The Virtue of Aging*, "There are two periods in our lives when we have exceptional freedom: at college age and when we begin our retirement years. At those times, we have relatively few restrictions and obligations..."[38]

Baby Boomers have always been a force to be reckoned with. You have redefined every stage of life thus far. Now you have an opportunity to re-define—or, hey, let's go bigger: *revolutionize*—retirement.

As a cohort, you are living a more active, longer retirement, and you have more options for making your retirement more meaningful than ever before. That means that the old story of retirement is no longer relevant for many of us. We're here to pursue a life of meaning and happiness, and for each of us that means a different thing. One thing is for sure, we will only find that authentic and fulfilling retirement when we override the preconceptions of retirement. It's your time to *rock* retirement.

False Advertising of the The Retirement Myth

Retirement isn't a new concept, but the way we think about it is. The first inklings of retirement began in 13 B.C.E., when Roman Emperor Augustus enacted a pension for soldiers that had served 20 years. It wasn't until 1881 that Prime Minister Otto Von Bismarck of Prussia proposed a financial assistance program to the elderly. It seemed outrageous at the time, since most people worked if they were able. Even the wealthy had to keep up management over their farms or property instead of having to work the farm. Once Germany was able to set retirement laws into motion eight years later, the rest of the world started to follow suit.

For America, non-military workers were able to get pensions during the 1920s if they worked in large industrial companies and hit 65. The Social Security Act joined us 15 years later, pegging retirement age for all at 65. At the time, the life expectancy of the average American male was 58. Today's picture is quite different. With the end of the Great Depression, life expectancy increased. With that increase in life expectancy—and wealth—rose our expectations of retirement. We developed the notion of a golf-and-margarita, American Dream-style retirement. With life expectancy on the rise, people enjoyed long retirements, and thus the idea of taking the time to relax was marketed to us. Now we have expanded retirement expectations even further: International and extended travel, dinners out, a wealth of experiences and relaxation. Nothing wrong with these things. What an incredible world and time we live in.

But somewhere along the way, the conversation became less about living a meaningful, fulfilling retirement and more about how much you can buy and do with your retirement. We see news reports about Baby Boomers not being financially positioned to retire, but we also have an expectation that we should be able to do more with our money.

There are two traits about modern day retirement I call for us all to challenge:

1. The commercialization of retirement.
2. The idea that there is a certain age to retire.

My first point sounds like it could be in conflict with my Retirement Revolution, right? Have I not just spent the first two parts of this book telling you that you can afford to spend more during your retirement, starting on the day you retire? (Assuming you have at least $200K saved and you are prepared to invest those funds.) The answer is yes. I'm holding true on my spending philosophy. My point is that in order to fully enjoy and get the most out of your retirement, you have to base that spending on a retirement plan—not a financial plan, but on a life plan.

Far be it from me to tell you how to spend your money, but I can't help but share how time and again I hear from retired folks about how dissatisfied they are with their retired life. Buying stuff and going out for dinner is nice, but does it lead to happiness or to a sense of fulfillment? My hope is that by empowering you to spend some of your savings, you'll uncover a meaningful retirement. Meaningful to you, not me, or the industries that want your retirement dollars.

It may sound appealing at first to lounge around for a few years after working so hard, but it's been so ingrained in us to think that that's what we *should* want. No one talks about how after those first couple of years, a lack of purpose can get dull. We all talk of wanting more time to relax after working hard for 40 years. But after a while, the need for meaning and purpose pops its head up time and time again. At least it does in my experience.

I talk with folks who have been retired from their work for years. They are typically retired doctors, attorneys, war veterans, business owners, teachers and nurses. Several of them tell me the biggest mistake they ever made was retiring as early as they did. Some have actually said, "Retirement sucks." They jumped the gun. When you look just about every one of them in their eyes, you can tell that they're a little upset that they have been sold a false bill of goods.

They've done everything correctly throughout their life. They've built wealth, raised a family and were responsible with their life and money. Now they're 68 and are bored out of their minds. They may have gotten their golf game down by a few strokes, but between courses, they're leaning heavily on their clubs. They feel like they've lost their purpose, and when that happens, starting to feel old creeps in.

Their health starts to deteriorate. It's not just soaking in the pool for too long that's making their wrinkles deeper. They're less active. A storm of depression can brew as they experience a loss of identity; the men feel as though they've lost their "breadwinner" role and now don't know what to do.

When I look to the research on the retirement blues, I can't help but be surprised at the lack of consistent data out there, because again and again, I hear the same retirement malaise in my office.

Who Says You Have to Retire at 65?

The second issue I have with the way we think about retirement is the idea that there is a particular age we should retire. Each of us has a unique health and wealth profile, which means the time we need to retire is different for each of us. Also unique to each of us is how passionate we are about our work, how much we are driven by our work, and how much of our identity is connected to our work.

According to the U.S. Census Bureau, the average age of retirement in 2017 was around 63 to 65 years old, depending on the state. Usually people choose this specific time to get certain benefits at the beginning of their retirement, but that doesn't mean that you have to. Some people retire in their 40s, others in their 70s or 80s. Others simply don't retire at all; they enjoy their work too much or feel as though they have to work. Retirement is a choice, after all.

What you choose to do in retirement is not just a matter of working or not working. There is a wide spectrum of choices available to you when designing a post-work set of life choices that activate and inspire you. Counselling psychologist Nancy Schlossberg is one academic who is really raising awareness among retirees about the vast amount of possibility that awaits. In her research, she has found many factors that lead to fulfillment, including the degree to which you plan for retirement and what your expectations are. Dr. Schlossberg has identified six psychological profiles that cover how most of us approach retirement. She details these profiles in her book, *Retire Smart, Retire Happy*.[39]

"Continuers"
People who keep on applying their existing skills and interests.

"Adventurers"
Folks who make the opportunity to start new endeavors.

"Searchers"
Individuals who explore new options by trial and error.

"Easy Gliders"
People who want unscheduled time.

"Involved Spectators"
People who care about the world but engage in a less active way.

"Retreaters"
Those who take time out to recoup and regroup, or, have given up on connecting to a sense of purpose. Retreating can be a good thing, or sign of struggle.

Dr. Schlossberg's research is interesting to me because it takes into account the many individual differences among today's retirees. All of us have our own drives, personalities and connections to work, community and hobbies. And our levels of engagement may change at different points in our lives, depending on many factors like health, yes, but also what fulfills us. What you choose to do is a reflection of what you value.

Some studies show that health declines in retirement for those who don't work;[40] others show that health and well-being outcomes improve with retirement.[41]

Researchers discuss how it's our relationship to work and our expectations of retirement, that can lead to our health and psychological well-being. If we love our work, and it makes us happy, and we are in good health, what is to stop us from continuing? If our work is unfulfilling and stressful, then retirement may feel like a relief. It's all down to our individual circumstances.

Recently, I met a man who had worked for the FBI for 30 years and had a pension he was required to take at a relatively young age. Hayden, as I'm going to call him, was done working at 55. Minus working at Home Depot making $9/hour, he doesn't have many employment opportunities with his very specific skill set. For the first six months of his retirement, Hayden got up, read the paper and went to the gym. He would come back home and it was only 11 a.m. When he came into my office, I could tell he was tired, but not from lack of sleep. His stare was dull.

"Dave, retirement's awful," Hayden said.

A lot of men are ashamed that they are feeling this way. They talked their whole lives about that golden age when they would be retired and finally happy. However, it just isn't the case. He couldn't think of a thing to do.

Another man, 62, came to my office. When he was 50, he sold his business for $30 million. He had not worked a day in the past 12 years. He looked old, at least 10 years older than he actually was. Gray hairs were thinning over his tanned head. Deep wrinkles hung around his sunken eyes like cobwebs. From the other side of my desk, he told me that if I had an opportunity to sell my business at a young age and retire early, I should refuse.

"I regret it," he said. "It's not even about the money anymore." He no longer felt like he had any purpose or meaning. He felt invisible.

My dad is 70 and still working. When he was 65, he considered selling his business and retiring. As he talked to his friends and saw what they were going through, he decided he was not going to sell.

Now he says it's one of his best decisions.

In American society, when you are retired you can feel like you are invisible. You are not part of the working world anymore. For some, those of us who are actively told by society to work hard, approaching the slower-paced, leisurely world of retirement can be disheartening.

A Cure for the Retirement Blues

Once I spoke with a woman who was married to a corporate executive for a large company. The day after he retired was one of her most heartbreaking days.

Her husband woke that morning, looked at her and said, "What do I wear?" The routine of waking up and putting on his suit was pointless now, since his time at the company was over. His entire identity had been wrapped up in his job, and he hadn't prepared for the day where he no longer had to wear a tie. His wife ended up finding some ways to keep him busy after a lot of trial and error.

She finally got him into researching the background of old homes in the area, using the resources at the county office. Once his hands were flipping through files again, he became much happier. He felt like he had a reason to get up. He was able to help people understand the history of their homes. With each person or couple that left his office, he felt as though he was finally able to contribute again.

The lesson here is that retirement and financial planning can only go so far. There's also life planning scenarios that movies, TV and periodicals won't likely cover or illustrate. Thankfully, we have professional retirement life coaches when we are stuck. And sometimes, financial advisors find themselves in the same role. If there is a life lesson that I have picked up from my retired client's, it's this: You don't *have* to retire.

We can't assume that when you stop working, everything is going to be golden, beautiful and perfect. For some, that may be the case. For others, maybe not, but that's alright, too.

You are not obligated to retire in the way the world tells you, if at all. All it takes is a little introspection and a stable financial plan.

Retirement is all down to your imagination. If you like to work, work! If you have another hobby you want to pursue, do it and do it with gusto! Working brings structure to life. Continuing to work, assuming that your work drives you and you love your work, is one way to keep engaged in the structures that bring us security and connection to the world around us. I'm not saying you have to continue with your work specifically, or to take paid work. I'm saying that retirement, as it is sold to us, is selling you short. You have skills, experience and energy to offer your community, country and world. And your community, country and world WANT YOU. It's all down to you and how you want to engage in the world. It's an exciting crossroads!

Whatever you do, it's your dream to make and your money to spend.

A lot of people end up retiring because they're forced into it, whether they're ready or not. I think tuning out those "ideal retirement" fantasies we see on billboards and TV will help us think about how to reinvent ourselves in retirement, and to see how to really make our retired years special. A big part of owning your retirement is through spending your money.

Rather, I should say *using* your money. *Intentionally applying* your money. Putting your money to work in a mindful fashion is paramount to an empowered retirement. You've got your financial plan in place to cover you for your "what ifs" like medical or long-term care expenses. The good news is that YOU *make* your best retirement, and you've got some cash to help you *reinvent your retirement.*

This is not your parents' retirement. Your life is not a retirement commercial. You have one of the most incredible opportunities: Not only do you have a solvent Social Security, you are financially positioned to LIVE an empowered retirement and to discover or develop talents and passions you might not have during your working life, or you have the opportunity to transfer your skills and passion for your work into a whole new realm, if not to continue working as you did before. In the era of the internet, and good financial planning, there is no good reason you should have a restricted retirement. You can use the tremendous opportunity we currently seem to be stuck calling "retirement" to fulfil your potential and dreams.

Retirement is a Series, not a Movie.

We often think of retirement as a block of time. But retirement is more than one stage of life. It's a series of stages and transitions. Just as any stage of life is. Your working life was defined by many different stages and experiences—retirement is no different. Your retirement will mean many things to you at different times. By taking the time now to take a look at your values, your desires, and the meaning you ascribe to your life, you have the opportunity to make a retirement living plan that allows you to uncover those ambitions and plans.

There is no pressure here. I'm not saying you have to go be Superman or Wonder Woman. I do want to say that the time just before you retire is a beautiful opportunity to contemplate, with a sense of purpose, what you want from your retirement.

If you've already retired, it's never too late to contemplate the opportunities and experiences you want to explore. When you have a true sense about what fulfills you, you are in a much better position to tell your investment advisor what you want him or her to accomplish for you and the money you intend to put to work while you pursue your purpose.

When you plan how you want your retirement to look in terms of stages, you open yourself up to wider possibilities. Ever heard of that time management tip on chunking down your time? When we chunk down our time, we make big, daunting tasks seem more manageable. I believe the same can be said for retirement. When we see retirement in stages, it's easier to envision our paths to fulfillment, for example, choosing to continue working, volunteering or mentoring. The options are endless, depending on our desire to work, engage and participate in our communities. Also, we know that those choices don't define our entire retirement; when we decide to continue working or volunteer or try a new business, we know it is for this particular stage of our retirement—it's just one part of our patchwork quilt, and there's zero pressure or requirement for a particular patch to last forever, unless you want it to.

Personally, I have no plans of ever retiring. I think I'll work as long as I can still stand. My work is just too interesting for me to want to leave it. I love working with people on their investments, and answering their questions about how to plan financially for their best lives. I can't *not* want to help. It's the palpable sense of relief I see in people. The lives transformed and changed. It is remarkably rewarding.

I consider myself lucky because I happen to have a job that I adore. It's not even a job; it's something that I would do anyway. If somebody asked me what I would want to do, I would tell them that I'd want to sit down with people and help them with their finances. That's what I like to do. Some people like to golf, some people like to fish. I like to sit down with people and help them bring their finances to life. I have four children, so I guess I still have to get paid, but in the end I want to help people through the retirement stage of life. Getting that paycheck is more or less a bonus.

If I could help clients figure out how to live their lives to the fullest and prove to them that it's okay to spend what they've earned, then I'd consider it a good day at the office. Being a financial advisor is more than a job, and more than a hobby; it's my calling.

I can't help but think of George Burns, whose acting career revitalized at the age of 79. He kept working until a few weeks before he passed away as a centenarian. He famously said, "Retirement at sixty-five is ridiculous. When I was sixty-five I still had pimples." If this is true for you too, then embrace your desire to work—even if going back to work means getting creative: Start your own business, be a consultant, or keep working at your place of business, if you can. There are plenty of ways to keep your hand and mind in the game. The world needs your experience. GO FOR IT!

Baby Boomers! *You are better prepared for retirement than almost any other generation.* You will retire at one of the most optimal times, with an intact Social Security, Medicare plans that deliver, and retirement plans you have diligently contributed to over the course of your lives. The Baby Boomer generation is wealthier than any other before it. Yes, there are plenty of Boomers who are not as financially secure as they would like to be. But the numbers don't lie, so let's revisit that Chapter 1 stat: Boomers make up 24 percent of the American population, while owning up to 80 percent of the nation's wealth (in a nation which owns 41.6 percent of the world's wealth!). Many of us have long retirements to look forward to, and even with 80 percent of Boomers facing a chronic health condition, Boomers are well positioned to be able to afford their retirements and their healthcare.

Now I am talking about you as a generation, and we all know that everyone's individual financial situation is unique. Whether you have a healthy retirement savings account or you don't, you still have an opportunity to redefine what retirement means to you — beyond the image of purposeless leisure that has been successfully marketed to you.

(This is where I add a long caveat about "purposeless leisure": Please don't take offense if that so-called "purposeless leisure" is exactly what you seek; if that's your mission, then do your thing, and do it with pride. I'm going to add a big "but" here. If you are just following what you believe to be the normal way of retirement, and you question that choice, and I think you might question the version of retirement that is sold to us if you are reading this book, then read on and explore the alternative!)

We are afforded amazing opportunities as a result of our good fortune to be born in, or to move to, a country in a time when we have retirement plans we can count on. The opportunities we have to develop ourselves are unparalleled. We have the opportunity to design our retirements—and its many transitions and stages—as we desire.

Retirement is an inspiring opportunity to reinvent ourselves.

Our choices are abundant. Whether you want to continue to work, to volunteer, or to take classes and develop yourself further, it's time to see retirement as the opportunity that it is. Especially when you have the option to invest in yourself and the things you think are important, by putting your savings to work. As you evaluate what it is you want to do with your retirement, I think it's of value to mention that making choices that connect you to the world around you are important. It might seem elementary, but all too often, folks turn up in my office with not much reason to leave the house other than to go to the grocery store or out to dinner.

That's why it's so crucial to put your own structure in place.

You are in Charge of Your Retirement.

We are under no requirement to be of service, but, in my experience finding a way to contribute to our communities is a source of great personal fulfillment. It's not an either/or game. You can design plenty of personal experience, joy and relaxation into your *self-directed* retirement. You call the shots.

In fact, capitalizing on the fact that you can add a pinch of travel, a pinch of family and a pinch of work or volunteering, to whatever degree you desire, is a pretty incredible position to be in.

A great example of how you can design a retirement that reflects you best is by my friend, Susan, whom you met earlier. For 40 years, Susan worked as a high school guidance counselor in Ohio. She retired at 65, on a good state teacher pension and her husband's pension (he had passed away 15 years earlier). Susan wasn't done working. She didn't want to get up at 5 a.m. to get her work done any more, as she had for the last 40 years, but *she did want to work.* So she did. She went back to work at the school. The time came when she did not have a choice but to retire. So she did. For about a week. At first, Susan felt like she had lost a piece of her identity. Who was she without her school? What surprised her most was how quickly she overcame this feeling. She opened her mind to the idea that there were all sorts of places to put her energy and intellect, of which she has an abundance. Susan doesn't call this post-work time "retirement;" she calls this period "the small stepping stones of life." She takes on each choice as "for now," and for as long it as feels right, she keeps going.

Susan became a full-time volunteer at her local church, working in the administrative office, but with an impact that was felt throughout her congregation. As a full-time volunteer, her experience and knowledge was highly valued and she enjoyed being part of a team working towards goals that she valued: her church's charitable missions, and community events. Susan took plenty of time for herself: taking breaks from Ohio winters with extraordinary travel experiences around the United States, and a cruise or two to the Caribbean. She had the perfect blend—for her—of working towards a meaningful goal like helping families in need, and taking time for herself. Susan said that now she enjoys the vast amount of freedom she has, because she has found a place where she can contribute and make a difference.

Family was and still is one of Susan's most important concerns; she is able to help take care of her critically ill granddaughter, and help out her kids here and there, which fulfills her *and* exhausts her sometimes—she cut back when it became too much. Susan also has changed her retirement schedule recently: Her latest stage of retirement sees her volunteering in Ohio from March until September, and taking in Florida's fine winters where she enjoys visiting friends, family and the parks. She's thinking about getting a job at Disney, because she enjoys the atmosphere so much, and she has plenty of energy for this kind of work. A giver at heart, Susan thoughtfully contributes to nonprofits she believes in, and helps organize local community events. After a double hip and knee replacement, Susan is leading an even more active and fulfilling retirement. She started to take more time for herself in the last few years, and she is proactive about making her days fulfilling in ways that are meaningful to her: She does her devotions, she helps her family out some, and she is catching up on reading, which she loves.

Are you Really Ready to Retire (in the Traditional Sense)?

We all think about work in our own unique way. If Susan's example resonates with you, it is worth asking yourself if you are ready to retire in the old-fashioned sense of the word. Now I know many people who say they just want to retire and live the high life, but invariably, absent any health constraints, retirees are looking for an antidote to boredom, and want to stay present in the world through work, volunteering, mentoring or developing a skill.

If you are looking for more in retirement, you are in good company. According to the aforementioned HRS Study, 43 percent of females and 50 percent of males return to work after retirement. PEW found that 18.8 percent of Americans over the age of 65 reported being employed full or part time.[42] Now, people go back to work for various reasons. Some of us have to continue working. Whether you choose to go back to work, or you have to, the internet has opened up legitimate opportunities for you to extend your professional experience into the consulting or "gig economy" realm—for example, if you are a writer, you can market yourself on LinkedIN or through contractor websites like Upwork; if you are skilled at handiwork, gardening or home organization, for example, websites like TaskRabbit and NextDoor connect you to opportunities in your community. Of course, there is also good ol' fashioned networking, and growing your consulting or home business through your existing and likely extensive professional network, perhaps even your former employer.

University of Florida researchers studied going back to work after retirement and came up with this great piece of advice that I feel resonates for those of us who just don't want to stop working yet.[43]

> *"Instead of viewing retirement as a career exit,*
> *it can be conceptualized as a late-career development stage."*

In another study, researchers found that those people who chose a "bridge" employment in their chosen careers—that is, a part-time or temporary position had better health and well-being outcomes than those who didn't. (And the researchers took into account existing health issues that might prevent someone from working in the first place.)[44]

One man who did change careers, and found the experience a very happy one, was a man named Brian; though his secret was that he never took it too seriously. Brian moved to the U.S. from England some 20 years ago. He retired comfortably and planned to live the high life. Then his wife passed unexpectedly. As he grieved, he was looking for ways to get out of the house. He took a chance on an "Extras Wanted" ad from a local theater group. He had nothing to lose. Little did he know that he would end up tapping into an unknown talent. Brian ended up being called back as a regular extra, and even got some named parts … with lines! We are talking about a person who had absolutely zero experience in the acting world. Nada. Zip. He went in with a laid- back attitude and no expectations, and lo and behold he ended up with a "late-stage career" he never imagined possible. Brian loves his work, and enjoys seeing work as a joy—something he chooses to do or not to do. Brian's serendipitous career ENERGIZES him. He has met some great people along the way, from all backgrounds and ages, which really excites him. In short: through his new work, Brian found a whole new lease on life.

Remember, my message is all about you making a retirement that makes you happy and overriding any preconceived ideas we have about a traditional linear retirement. You might not *need* to work. But there is no rule in the world that says you can't. Work if it fulfills you. Start a business, if you are so driven. Go forward and never stop growing. (Side note: if you are claiming Social Security, and you are under 66, you need to pay attention to how much you are earning—pop back to Chapter 9 for more information.)

The Power of Volunteering

Retirees who volunteer report higher levels of health and well-being, not to mention a sense of purpose and self-esteem. It turns out Baby Boomers are master volunteers. According to the National Corporation for Community Service, Baby Boomers make up some 30 percent of the nation's volunteers.[45] Your generation may volunteer for their place of worship, which is the most common place for volunteer work, but there are lots of other options. Baby Boomers are a well educated group, and as a result education is the second largest venue for volunteers. There are organizations calling out for your skills. And when I say skills I mean professional level skills. Managerial, organizational and administrative skills are called for, as are mentor, tutor and teaching skills. Your abilities and experience are very much in demand: mentorship, a listening ear, NICU baby holding—you name it. There's a wide world calling for your experience and judgment.

Depending on your personal interests and skills, there are a wealth of opportunities available to you. If you are interested in sharing your business skills, connect with your local business incubator or SCORE, a business mentor program. If you want to mentor a child who could use a good role model, Big Brothers Big Sisters are calling out for volunteers, particularly men. If you are looking for a more global volunteering opportunity, you might consider a church mission trip, or exploring opportunities with one of the many international volunteering organizations—some of whom specialize in connecting retirees to volunteer experiences.

Replenish, Reinvent, Reinvigorate!

Retirement, as we like to call it, is really an opportunity to grow and expand our horizons, rather than limiting and contracting ourselves. It's all about mindset. How you think about life, and your values, what is important to you and your openness to possibilities—that's all in your mindset. We are happiest when we live out our authentic dreams and wishes.

What will your post-work mindset look like? Write down what you want from your retirement and explore what your possibilities might be. Don't hold back. There are no crazy ideas.

Ask yourself:

- What do you want to give **yourself**?
(Perhaps you need to take care of yourself instead of others for a while, to restore your well-being after working hard. Perhaps you are ready to take skydiving lessons or to prep for your next marathon. Whatever it is you need to do for yourself, and you are driven to do, write it down and explore it, knowing that you can budget for it with your five percent spending money!)

- Do **your partner, family or people you love** have a need that you are committed to supporting?
(Ask how your partner's or family's needs factor into your day-to-day, ability/will to work or volunteer. Is there a part of couple or family life you want to nurture, now that you have more time? Family might mean friends—the people you hold near and dear.)

- Is there a **skill** you've always wanted to develop?
(Such as art, music, writing, woodwork, starting a radio show or podcast— the options are endless.)

- How are you a part of your **community**?
[We all need a connection to our community, especially when we stop going out to work each day. How do you see yourself being a part of your community? Do you have skills that can be put to work (hint: you very most likely do, even if you don't know it). Is there a problem in your community (or in another community or even a country) to which you believe you can be of service?]

In Chapter 12, we are going to look at concrete ways you can put your five percent spending money to work. Whether you want to spend your savings on yourself, your family, the wider community or a cause you care about. There has never been an easier time to connect with the causes and experiences that mean the most to you. This is your time to redefine what retirement means to you. Whether you are embracing the idea of a "late-career" position or "bridge" employment, or whether or not you want to volunteer, or start a business, there are no rules when it comes to your retirement. Remember, as we said before, we chunk down our retirement and start to see our possibilities. What do you see for your first year of retirement? Do you have a specific goal—even if that goal is to relax as much as possible!? And then think longer-term and bigger picture; what gives you fulfillment and meaning? It might be learning or developing a photography passion, volunteering at your local school, or coaching fellow Boomers to live their best retirement. Once you have your bigger picture goals in mind, chunk them back down into small steps so you can accomplish the retirement you desire.

When you do know what you want to do with the next year, five years, and beyond, tell your advisor what you seek to accomplish, and ask him or her to devise a spend plan that fits your budget. You are going to do amazing things with that five percent spending money!

CHAPTER TWELVE:

See The Fruits Of Your Labor In Action Now

We make a living by what we get,
but we make a life by what we give.
Winston Churchill

There is a common question that pops up in my practice, once clients get used to receiving their budgeted spending money each month. Often clients have an extra $2,000, and even $5,000 extra, a month. A not insignificant number of clients receive an extra $10,000 or $20,000 a month. At first, clients will treat themselves perhaps to a new kitchen, a car or an incredible vacation; but invariably, the big question arises again and again:

"What do I do with all this extra money?"

It's a good question, and the answer is different for each of us. We all have our unique passions and drives. I feel that, for someone who has really assessed what they want from retirement, the answer might pop into their head right at this moment. If you are not sure yet what you want to do with your extra spending money, you have a great opportunity to think about how your retirement expenditure reflects your values and beliefs. I urge people to think about how they want to pay their money forward as part of their retirement planning, because it is way more satisfying to see the incredible feats your money can accomplish. Here and now.

In this chapter we will talk about some of the concrete ways you can invest in yourself, but also how you can "pay it forward."

Put Your Money to Work for the Things You Care About

I'm a financial advisor, not a life coach or a therapist, and far be it from me to tell you how to spend your money. You might well know exactly how to spend your money, once you empower yourself to withdraw some of those extra beans. Still, over the years talking with clients and folks in my Social Security classes, I've seen many different ways retirees engage their funds to live a fulfilling life. Your best choices for spending your money will come from your own heart and vision, so take these ideas purely as a source of inspiration, or as talking points. Or take them and run with them!

There are five main areas where you can put your money to work for your best retirement: Health, yourself, family, community and philanthropy.

#1. Health: Body and Mind

Whether you are about to retire, or you have been retired for a while, now is your chance to use time and money to take care of yourself. Join the YMCA, or a health club; and hire a personal trainer, golf instructor or private yoga teacher. Buy quality, healthy food or even get yourself a personal chef or nutritionist. You might even consider hiring yourself a concierge doctor. If you have the funds to invest in your health now, your future self and your future bank account will likely thank you.

Psychological Planning for Big Transitions

Mental health is just as important as physical health. Invest in your psychological well-being by hiring a coach or counselor, if you feel like you would like one, or join groups who support you in finding your identity and purpose in retirement. I'm amazed at the number of clients who would never dream of spending the money on getting therapy support for their day-to-day challenges, be they marital, personal or professional.

Yet, the more we learn about retirement, we more we learn about the many transitions that accompany the post-work life. Nancy Schlossberg, the retirement psychologist I referenced prior, talks about how our "roles, routines and relationships" change through the many transitions in retirement. Those three "Rs" of retirement are pretty powerful when you stop to think about them; what we now do with our time, how we find our purpose and how all this affects our relationships— there is a lot to talk about when we want to live our best retirement. Part of having good health is taking care of our mental and emotional well-being.

#2. Give to Yourself

As the great Warren Buffett said, *"The most important investment you can make is in yourself."* You have the funds and the time, so embrace the opportunity to nurture and develop yourself. You can afford to do nice things for yourself. It's all part of the balance. We work, we contribute and lift up our communities, *and* we take care of ourselves. You are providing opportunities and employment to others when you "spoil yourself," so go ahead, buy the kitchen, get the massages, buy the awesome golf clubs. Hire a writing teacher, or take acting classes, or sign up with your local university. Join the wide array of clubs in your local area, be it through your recreation center, the library, through MeetUp, or other groups you find online.

And travel! Whether you take a river cruise through Germany, a cruise through the Panama Canal or an RV trip around the United States, the options are obviously boundless. I won't turn this book into a travel brochure, but explore your options—you can travel … you get to see the world out there!

Your Investment Gives and Gives Again

Your investment in yourself is an investment in all the people that help you along the way. As much as you are investing in yourself, you are investing in your local and wider economy, injecting your money back into the world. I hear feedback from clients saying that they don't feel comfortable spending money on themselves, that they are being selfish. It's usually these folks who are the furthest thing from selfish.

Part of designing your retirement according to your personal desires is being connected to the idea that you have earned every penny you own, and when you spend with considered intention, you are not wasting a single penny. You are lifting up those you pay, directly and indirectly, as you spend. This is obviously true whether or not you are retired, but I want to mention this notion because retirement is an opportunity to participate and contribute, not to retract.

Our post-work money is still working for us, so it is still plenty able to engage in the world, just as it did when we worked. The only difference is that you don't have to actually work anymore.

#3. Family: Here and Now

As we discussed in Chapter 10, if you want to give to family, "giving while living" allows you to see the profound and positive impact your money can have on your heirs. You have the ability to ensure your money is spent wisely, and for sound benefit. You also have an opportunity to use your hard-earned savings to nurture connections and elevate your family members at key points in their lives, at times when they could use the support. When giving through a will, the money might well be useful, but it won't necessarily be strategically put to work for maximum benefit.

Seeing your money make a difference to the people you love is deeply satisfying. You might be able to get your sibling back on their feet after a job loss, or get your grandkid tutoring or piano lessons that would otherwise be out of reach. One client of mine funded his daughter's college education, financially helping her all the way to medical school, ultimately helping her become a neurosurgeon. Others started traditions of renting vacation homes each year to bring the family together for a few weeks over the summer. You get the combined benefit of amazing views *and* quality time with children and grandchildren!

#4. Contribute to Your Community

Contributing to your community, or another community you care about, is a meaningful way for you to create opportunities for the next generation. You might choose to contribute to your community as a sponsor of special arts and cultural events, or as a sponsor of a local school.

For those of us who like the idea of investing in the future—in individuals or projects we believe in—there are a number of legitimate crowdfunding websites that allow you to do so. Mainstream examples include KickStarter for creative projects, DonorsChoose for educational projects, or Experiment.com to invest in scientific research. The beauty of the crowdsourcing platforms that are available is that we are all able to pool together our resources to accomplish big things. Of course, you can always accomplish plenty in your community the old-fashioned way, while participating in your community in person!

#5. Giving While Living—About Time!

It takes money to make things better in this world. And action, and love. But money is definitely required.

There's a shift coming in how we pay our gifts and rewards forward as a population. I, for one, am relieved and glad. I write about spending your retirement savings because I grew tired of seeing clients not enjoying their hard-working retirement funds.

Sometimes unused money went forward to family. Sometimes left-over money was paid forward, according to their wishes, in a way that would be tremendously meaningful to the individual. Of course, there were other times when folks had not made plans for their money after they had gone, and that is a whole other story.

I'm always humbled by the experience of seeing retirement accounts becoming bequests. But I also find it sad that some of my clients didn't see first-hand the impact their gifts had and continue to have on their beneficiaries, especially when I know how much they cared.

That's why I am glad we have role models like Bill and Melinda Gates and Warren Buffett who have set up foundations in their lifetimes to which they give now, in addition to pledging their entire fortunes to the missions to which they are personally connected. They are starting long-overdue conversations about seeing the "fruits of your labor" put to work now, while you are here. Of course, the investment industry talks about philanthropic giving, but let's not forget advisors are incentivized to keep your money invested for as long as possible. Of course, you will keep plenty invested so that a constant income stream keeps flowing for each stage of your retirement. What you will be able to do is give monthly gifts according to your budget and the "annual five percent" you will receive each month. We will still have money to invest and grow, while we make a difference, now.

It doesn't take giving away millions and billions of dollars to make a difference, of course. We don't have to set up foundations. But if we do have the intention to support our chosen causes, or to support family, giving as we can afford to while we are here lets us:

a) Enjoy seeing what happens when we pay forward our wealth
b) Ensure our funds are used as we hope

"I Spent the Money ... and it Feels Awesome."

My personal favorite example of a retiree using their five percent spending money to realize a dream is Gina. Gina's vision made a massive impact on hundreds of people's lives, and accomplishing her dream turned out to be a transformative experience for her.

At first, Gina resisted the idea of spending her five percent, but once she saw how much she had in her account, relative to how much she was spending, she changed course. Some months later, we sat down to our review appointment. It was then she told me how she had spent the budgeted spending money she had accumulated.

"I grew up in a farmhouse in Pennsylvania. My grandfather built our family home with his own hands, and I can't tell you how much I loved it. Last year, I paid a visit to see the house I was raised in. Imagine my shock when I saw on the door a "No Trespassing" sign, the house falling down around it, the lawn overgrown and disheveled. The house was now on the bank's books, and no one was taking care of it."

Gina paused, and then I caught a spark in her eye. "Dave, I bought the house."

Right away, she hired a contractor and fixed the house up like new, as she remembered it, right down to the cream, floral wallpaper. Gina could have kept the house, or sold it, so what she did next blew me away. She donated the whole property to her local domestic violence center, which she had always supported. Her meticulously restored childhood home became a place of safety for domestic violence survivors and their children. Just think about how many people have escaped abusive partners and found shelter, thanks to her gift.

Gina empowered herself to use her spare money to restore a place of meaning to her, to continue her grandfather's legacy of having built a family home, and in doing so she created her own legacy: a sanctuary for those in the most desperate of situations. In total, her project cost her $80,000. She got to see her money in action, and she still kept $600,000 in her savings, which continues to work for her.

Chapter Thirteen:

The Couple That Plans Well Together, Spends Joyfully Together

You can align your values with your dreams and live a fulfilling life ... if you and your partner work on this money stuff together
David Bach

Frank, a retired police officer, met with his financial advisor several times right before he retired. Together, they assembled the multiple pieces of his financial puzzle, taking into account his income streams from Social Security and retirement plans. They discussed at length how to invest his, and his wife's, retirement savings, which were very healthy.

The BIG problem was that Frank's wife, Barbara, never attended a single meeting with their advisor. Frank handled all major financial decisions and that was that. Barbara handled the day-to-day budget of groceries and general living expenses. She knew how much was in the checking and she knew how much savings they had, she just didn't get involved in the management of their money. This was just the way Frank and Barbara operated.

So at 65, Frank hung up his badge and settled into retirement. Having spent time with his advisor, Frank thoroughly understood that a diversified portfolio of stocks and bonds was a powerful and consistent way for his money to make money. He knew that he had an additional recurring monthly income to complement his Social Security and his pension plan payments. He also was very clued in to how much he needed each month, and how his health expenses would not spiral out of control thanks to the out of pocket maximums of his and Barbara's Medicare plans.

Frank got it. He understood that it was OK to start spending his hard-earned savings now that he was retired. The man had big plans, and he knew exactly how to put them to work. Top of the list was to buy an old boat and fix it up. He couldn't wait to take on the project and to feel the satisfaction of making a great-looking boat for him, his wife and his friends to enjoy. Frank also knew that he and Barbara could vacation in the Caribbean for a few weeks each year, or wherever took their fancy now that they had all this freedom. Joining the local country club where all of his golf buddies hang out was also high on his list.

"Barb," Frank said, one day as they were drinking their morning coffee together, "I'm thinking about checking out a nice bass boat I saw online."

Barb's eyes widened and stared at her husband incredulously. "What do you mean!? We can't afford that!"

Barb couldn't believe that Frank, who had always been so careful with money, was now talking about spending thousands on fixing up a boat. They were on a fixed income now, and Barbara felt fearful about the their funds running out now that Frank was not working. In fact, she didn't really have any of her own goals or dreams for her own retirement, as Frank did; she had dismissed any ideas of vacations or special projects she, herself, might be interested in. The fact that Frank was talking about buying a boat felt like lunacy.

Frank responded matter of factly, "Don't worry about it. We are fine. My advisor says that we can spend nearly $3,000 a month from our savings, above and beyond our budget. They are only asking about $10,000 for the boat. I have it all figured out. We can afford it."

Barb shot back, "Are you out of your mind, Frank? The news last night said the Dow Jones went way down. And you know what? Nancy next door keeps talking about this stuff she's reading online. She is positive that the economy is about to collapse. Frank, there is no way we can be spending money on stuff like this."

Frank saw the look in his wife's eye, and knew she meant business. He also saw the wide gulf between Barb's beliefs about retirement, and the concrete financial facts he had been privy to in his meetings with his advisor. That said, while he might not be the first to admit it, even though he had sat down with his advisor, he still didn't *totally* believe he could count on his savings or his careful budget. Perhaps Barb was right. His dreams of trolling the Gulf began to fade away. He called his advisor to tell him to reinvest any income from his savings. At the end of the day, he knew logically that he could afford to spend from his savings, but that underlying "what if" mentality grew like a weed when it met his wife's concerns.

Moral of the Story: If you are married, be sure to include your spouse in any financial planning discussions. I don't care if you usually handle "this kind of stuff." If you aren't on the same page as your spouse, you may end up like Frank, sitting on the sofa, watching a show about fishing and dreaming of what could have been.

The Importance of Financial Alignment in Marriage.

Many of my clients are couples, and I've noticed over the years that I have to make a point to ensure that both spouses attend our meetings. I explicitly state that we need both spouses present. Why? Even in this day and age, it's still the case, at least in my experience, that men are making many of the financial decisions. It's one thing when one member of the couple makes the financial choices, but to have one half of your duo not know what's going on financially, that's a whole other problem.

Couples might already share differing values about spending and saving, and I feel that at least some of the time, it's not just down to differences related to being male or female, but also down to not having the same set of facts. Different philosophies about how to put your money to work can stem from varying levels of financial education and experience, and sometimes just a lack of open communication about money can lead to a lack of alignment. In my experience, and I am aware there is a significant shift in gender equality in play, I find that men are still the leaders of finances in marriages. Often I find that, among married couples, the wives are typically less engaged in money management altogether.

Being financially aligned as a couple is a critical component of smart retirement planning.

1. Your Sense of Meaning in Retirement Can Depend on Financial Alignment.

As we saw in Frank and Barbara's story, both spouses needed to be informed about their financial reality. In their case it was so that they could align on their spending habits to accomplish some dreams—while not all dreams cost money, many do. The fact that Frank couldn't, or didn't, spend as they could afford meant that he had to give up on a dream he had transformed into a real and tangible goal. For Frank and Barbara, had they both understood how their portfolio worked, their retirements' meaning and purpose would be on a completely different path. Had Frank gone ahead and spent against his wife's wishes, you can imagine the discord that might result.

The alternative is that both members of the marriage should be equally informed, even when one spouse doesn't feel like they understand finances. Everyone can understand how their portfolio works, and your advisor should be more than happy to make sure that you *both*:

a) know your wealth management strategy and income.

b) align on how your account is managed.

c) support each other's dreams, goals and values.

Dr. John Gottman, a famous couples therapist, has found that money is one of the six main areas of marital conflict.[46] I love what he has to say about financial planning and shared meaning because an important message in *this* book—second only to the fact that 50 percent of Boomers can afford to spend five percent of their retirement savings each year—is that real retirement planning can only happen when you have a sense of meaning about what you want from your retirement. As Gottman states in his book, *The Seven Principles for Making Marriage Work*, "... work as a team on financial issues" and "express your concerns, needs and fantasies to each other before coming up with a plan."

2. Partners in Everything, Including Money.

In his book *Smart Couples Finish Rich*, David Bach[47] exchanges the term "spouse" for "partner," and I appreciate why he does this. It's really important to see each other as financial partners, regardless of who is or has been the breadwinner, or the person who has traditionally taken care of the finances. Seeing your spouse as your partner is key to being financially aligned, and key to successful investing for both of your retirements.

When both partners are engaged in wealth management, even if one partner knows more than the other, you have a much better starting point for talking about how you will spend your money.

I was not surprised when I learned from wealth psychology expert Kathleen Burns Kingsbury, that only 38 percent of couples see their advisor jointly.[48] She expands to explain that even in this day and age, women do not as frequently as men have a seat at the financial table, which, as I mentioned, I also find to be the case.

The only way there can be a retirement revolution, in my mind, is if both men and women are present in their retirement planning. Your own retirement portfolio will reflect the benefit of both your inputs. And your advisor will be better able to manage your portfolio investments when understanding what both of you want from your money, and what you expect of your retirement.

The other benefit of being money partners is the stronger connection you get to develop with your spouse. I've certainly found it to be the case. You are much more likely to explore the possibilities of what you want from life when you both understand the financial underpinnings of what's available to you.

Money touches practically every aspect of our lives, and like it or not, money is directly related to us living out our dreams, accomplishing our goals, and giving as we want. When together you share financial awareness, you are much better positioned to fully embrace the opportunities retirement affords. Understanding your money as partners helps you do the REAL retirement planning: How you will live and what you will do, together and for yourselves.

3. Preparing the Surviving Partner for a Secure and Thriving Life.

The other reality is that one partner will likely outlive the other, perhaps by a number of years. You want the less financially-engaged partner to be at least as empowered as the financially-engaged partner. A surviving partner should be prepared, and feel some security, not just from knowing there is some kind of financial plan in place. But also both partners should understand why choices were made and what income they have, and can expect to have at different stages of retirement. Both partners should understand the strategy that was set for when eligibility changes arise: for example, what happens to your Social Security upon the death of your partner—that's all part of the strategy you and your advisor put in place when you first set up your retirement plan.

We all have the capacity to understand how our financial plans work. It's not as complicated as we might tell ourselves. If we have never talked about our investments or financial plans, it naturally has the potential to be intimidating and overwhelming. A good advisor will guide you step by step through everything you need to know regarding your post-work income and your investment strategy. A good advisor will start where you are and explain anything that is new to you, or you want to understand better.

It's important to use an advisor with whom you share a good connection. If you have the sense that your advisor will take the time to answer your questions and to keep you up-to-date on what you need to know, then you are in a much better position. It's common for widows to change advisors upon the deaths of their spouses, and not at all surprising. By necessity, many widows start to take charge of their finances, if they were not involved before. Would it not be better to engage with your money manager from Day One of your retirement? I believe the continuity of the advisor-client relationship in times of turbulence is in your best interest, assuming you have a good advisor—all your plans are in place with your trusted financial guide, according to *both* of your wishes.

A Special Note to Women

There is a long-studied financial literacy gap between women and men, with women traditionally lagging behind in having the knowledge needed to make informed financial decisions. The good news is that gap is getting smaller and smaller for Boomers. Perhaps this reflects the fact that more Boomers, male and female, are paying more attention to their investments as they near retirement.

A study by FINRA, the U.S. broker-dealer regulator, recently showed that the financial literacy gap between men and women is 19 percent. That's higher than other generations: For example, with Millennials, the gender gap is 10 percent (though Millennials are less well informed in general than Boomers).[49]

As you would expect, the more educated and wealthier the woman, the more likely she is to be financially literate. In homes where women are the primary financial decision makers, they are more likely than male decision makers to have full retirement planning in place, for example: Social Security planning, health care expenditure and an investment income strategy.[50]

There are plenty of women who are clearly doing just fine, but I want to take a moment to address the women who do not feel connected to their retirement planning. The reality is that this information applies to *everyone* who does not feel connected to all things financial.

The American College of Financial Services recently released a study on financial literacy and women.[51] The researchers noted a financial literacy gender gap, though women are just as likely as men to have a financial advisor. The good news is that women typically expect more education and explanation from their advisor. The bad news with this study was that financial literacy and retirement planning are closely related. Many women are not planning for retirement as they should be. The study also found that as women typically live longer than men, their money often has to go further: They might have longer-term health expenses, for example. For this reason, I hope that more women will make a point to educate themselves or get good advisors who will educate while managing portfolios.

The Surviving Spouse's Guide to Retirement

These tips apply to both men and women, generally speaking. It's a good idea to make a financial plan in the instance that one partner outlives the other, though I appreciate it's not the top of everyone's to-do list. In the long run, planning now brings comfort when you need it.

#1. *Choose an advisor carefully.*

If you don't have an advisor already and you want one, then ask for referrals from trusted friends. Skip the "free steak dinners" and any calls you get from advisors that just heard you received a life insurance payout. When you do select an advisor, and you know you need education as well as financial management, make sure your connection with the advisor is good. You are paying your advisor, so feel empowered to ask as many questions as you see fit when selecting an advisor and gaining financial knowledge.

#2. *Get savvy on Social Security benefits.*

Social Security is particularly kind to surviving spouses, when done right. Generally speaking, a surviving spouse should claim the survivor benefit as soon as possible and let their own benefit grow and defer until age 70. Then, he or she can switch to their own, for a potentially larger benefit check. If the deceased spouse possessed a much larger Social Security benefit, then the strategy is different. In that situation the surviving spouse should take his or her own benefit as soon as possible. Then consider switching to their husband or wife's survivor benefit at age 66. Reference Chapter 9 for more in-depth Social Security information.

#3. *Make financial education empowering.*

If your spouse took care of your financial planning, and you need and want to know more, go straight to reasoned, objective sources of information. You know to skip the scary news headlines and to NOT follow the stock market every day. Take a finance or personal finance class at your local university, or find a trusted fiduciary who can serve as a coach, mentor or advisor.

#4. Override scarcity mentality

Overriding scarcity mentality is pretty much the premise of this entire book, but it's especially true for surviving spouses. It's easy to embrace a spending philosophy when you are a fearless duo. When we look at our income and finances as an individual, we might feel differently, even though we still have a relatively solid income. We might actually be better off, in financial terms.

We all know that most fear is not rational, however. And it is quite natural to question the abundance of our assets relative to our expenses, when we don't have our spouse to reassure us and reaffirm the merits of our approach.

Be steadfast in your conviction. Empower yourself to understand your investment income and the solidity of your other income streams, such as Social Security and pension plans. You have every reason to continue with your empowered retirement, continuing to spend five percent of your savings each year, as you see fit. Financially, you are STILL better off than you think.

#5 Connect with your people

Ask for help when you need it. You'll be surprised at how many people know what you are experiencing. I've certainly found this to be the case. With regards to financial well-being, if you are part of a group that shares your retirement philosophy of living with purpose and connection to what matters to you, then invite more of that in to your life. Spend more time with friends who align with you on living a meaningful retirement. Even better, if you have your own 5 Percent Club, which we will talk about in Chapter 14, you might just have a team of friends to anchor your sense of security and conviction when you need it.

Ways to Get Financially Aligned

I get that there is a challenge is changing the status quo, if you have spent the last 25 years of your marriage with one partner not engaged in finances. I have found among couples who have addressed their financial partnership imbalance that it can be a great opportunity to strengthen a bond and understand each other.

Some concrete ways to get financially aligned:

1. Book your first JOINT appointment with your financial advisor.

Explain to your advisor your intention that both partners understand their portfolio, and why they can afford to spend their five percent. Commit to both being present at your quarterly or annual meetings. Make sure that both partners feel able   to ask any question, even if one is more experienced than the other—the old adage applies here: There are no stupid questions.

2. Do the exercises in Part Two together.

Sit down together and work through the budget items, line by line so that you both get a chance to review your expenditures. Also sit down together to collect all your income sources and important documents. This is a team project. It also gives you the opportunity to review some of your expenses and ask together, do our spending choices reflect how we want to live, or do our expenses not reflect what actually makes us happy? (It's a great financial spring-cleaning opportunity, and gives the option to think more about what you want in life.)

3. Talk about your money mindsets.

What are your beliefs about money? Compare how you were raised when it comes to understanding money. Do you both carry a "Depression-era mentality" from your parents? Knowing where your individual and joint relationships with money come from is empowering. Do you have fears—the same or different? You might learn something new about your partner, or at least reconnect.

4. Talk about your dreams, goals and values.

If you could spend say, five percent of your savings each year, what would you do with it? This is the fun part, because it's REAL. You know the dollar amount of your five percent spend. If you have, say $3,000 a month like Frank and Barb, it's pretty exciting what you can do with that spending money, however you want to spend it! For some couples, it feels like a little lottery win.

Here's to making beautiful, spend-empowered retirements happen, together!

Chapter Fourteen:

Are YOU Ready to Join the Five Percent Club?

THANK YOU for taking this revolutionary ride through retirement with me. I hope that my message resonates and rings true with you.

By now, if you think like me, you are hopefully feeling empowered to live your most awesome retirement, according to *your* rules and dreams. You also might feel like the first duck to leave the old river in search of thriving waters.

If you do feel that way, know this: You are one of the first to participate in a general shift in thinking. There's a change happening in today's retirement zeitgeist, thanks to the Boomers. Lots of people are starting it *get* it. The folks at my Social Security classes get it. The investment industry is starting to get it, or at least some are starting to embrace the idea that you CAN spend during retirement. There is plenty of data to support the idea that you can spend more than you think in retirement. Now we just need to get our heads in the game. And to get our heads in the game, it helps to have a community that gets it.

You need your people—the people who get the five percent spend mentality—in your life.

When it comes to living your most YOU-driven retirement, it helps to know people who are going into the post-*official*-work life with the same level of fearlessness, intention and ACTIVATION!

That's why I created the 5 Percent Club.

The 5 Percent Club is really a mindset, rather than a club. Though I do have dreams of the 5 Percent Club becoming a country-wide— and hey, why not world-wide— community that lets you connect with folks who have the five-percent-spend mindset.

My hope is that people share their stories to inspire. Each of us who is learning about the profound impact there is in spending five percent of your savings each year will benefit from hearing trailblazer stories. Are you one of those revolutionary trailblazers?

If you have a take on rejuvenating retirement, I hope you will share your knowledge and experience. You are in a position to *reimagine* the abundant possibilities available to you in this new life stage of freedom and discovery. If you feel inclined to pay that experience forward, the 5 Percent Club is a good way to do it!

Be inspired by folks who activated their retirement dreams by empowering themselves to smart-spend their savings.

*And, in turn, **inspire forward!***

If you followed the exercises in Part Two of this book, you have a smart budget in place. You also might have an investing plan that allows you to spend five percent of your savings a year on the things that matter to you. Or you at least have the knowledge required to ask your advisor to create an income-bearing investment strategy *... that allows you to spend five percent of your savings a year on the things that matter to you.*

You know that there is plenty of historical data to support your ability to spend some while the bulk of your portfolio grows. Remember that Rolling Periods report in the Appendix? Check it out. It's there for your review whenever you want the reminder.

You can spend five percent of your savings each year—for your *entire* retirement.

From DAY ONE. We are not talking about spending during the "live large" years of retirement, but also the slower years (*if* you ever *really* slow down, that is).

I'm thinking that if you have come all the way through this book, you might just be ready to consider yourself a fully fledged member of the "5 Percent Club."

This is no elite club reserved only for those folks who saved a cool million for their retirement. The 5 Percent Club is open to everyone who saved at least $200,000 in retirement savings. That's nearly *half* of today's retirees.

There are 46 million Americans aged over 65, so there are approximately 23 million people in the United States today who have enough money saved to join the 5 Percent Club. That's incredible. Some *23 million* people in America have the means to spend five percent of their retirement savings each year. That's a lot of money that could be injected into the economy, and a lot of dreams being lived!

The 5 Percent Club Core Values

Those of us who identify as 5 Percent Club members align ourselves with a few core values, values which really reflect our mindsets of thinking for ourselves and having faith in our decisions.

The 5 Percent Club is Fearless.

The 5 Percent Club is made up of Baby Boomers who reject fear-based financial rhetoric. No matter from whence they hear the old "buy gold," and the "biggest recession to date is coming" talk, they are in charge of how they feel about their money. If someone on the TV, radio or internet says something about the financial markets that makes your heart beat faster, and your breaths feel shorter, the likelihood is that getting you to react that way is their goal. It's much easier to sell to you when you are scared. Reject it. Override the feeling fear-based advertisements and radio shows create with your historical perspective, and the knowledge that you have a sound, long-term financial plan in place. Override any emotional hangovers from being raised by Depression-era parents, if you are feeling that hangover. Be fearless, 5 Percent Club!

The 5 Percent Club is Diversified and Diverse!

Each Baby Boomer in the 5 Percent Club has invested their retirement savings in a diversified portfolio of stocks and bonds. Each *individual's* investment portfolio might have different individual stocks and funds, but the *asset allocation* will be about the same: That means that 5 Percent Club members will have at least 50 percent of their retirement assets in stocks, and the rest in bonds. Each portfolio might be diverse and reflect our individual values, *and* the specific advice of our financial advisors for our unique situations. In general, however, the allocation of asset classes will be along the same lines. All the 5 Percent Club people get INCOME from their portfolio, in the form of dividends, interest and growth. The market may go up and down but in the long-run, they will be able to withdraw five percent of their retirement portfolio balance each year.

The 5 Percent Club Folks Lead a Fulfilling, Self-directed Retirement

Each person in the 5 Percent Club lives and spends without fear, or a sense of scarcity. They have mindsets that allow them to explore just how much more colorful retirement can be when we unleash some of that saved cash. They know exactly how much spending money they have, once all the necessities are paid for. With that spending number in mind, they make empowered and secure choices about travel, education, pursuing a hobby or sport, giving ... in short, living the life they imagined. Your retirement money is sitting there waiting for you to put it to work on an awesome retirement. If you don't want to spend it on yourself, you can make a difference to others: Send your grandkids to camp or to music lessons ... or even college! Start a nonprofit, or donate to causes you care about. You are in the 5 Percent Club if you create opportunities for yourself to realize dormant dreams, or to connect with causes that are important to you.

The 5 Percent Club Knows There is No Such Thing as 100 percent Guaranteed.

The five-percent-spend approach is a sound financial choice, and we of the 5 Percent Club are aware of the reliability of annualized returns *over time*. As we learned in Part One, there has never been a time in modern economic history when a diversified portfolio of stocks and bonds does not return at least an annual return of 5 percent.

Want me to sign an affidavit guaranteeing with 100 percent certainty that the markets will return at least five percent in perpetuity? I'm about as likely to do that as a meteorologist is when predicting the weather, or any other specialist making a prediction for that matter. But the historical data is on our side of the argument. Some folks even go back as far as the 1800s to demonstrate the relative reliability of stock returns, over time. Stocks and bonds have been around that long and have shown a remarkable track record. Each year the world revolves around the sun, new developments emerge, but time and time again, the market recovers from downturns and, over time, grows. The only instance I can imagine that not happening, is if the world came to an end. And do we really think that is going to happen? Seriously!

The 5 Percent Club Make a Plan, Stick to it and then ROCK Retirement!

We go forward, knowing that we have made the best set of financial decisions possible, based on data, and based on listening to rationality over fear. We refuse to worry about running out of money; we educate ourselves about investing and staying the course. We will not be staying up late watching a talking head tell us that the financial markets are coming to an end. We don't get pinged by our phones each time the market moves. We have faith in the long run. We know that because we have made a sound investment plan that is working for us, and that our focus should be on rocking our retirements, according to our own personal drives and values!

Five Steps to Being 5 Percent Club Eligible!

It's easy to do, and free. There's no sign up or signing your life away. There are five simple steps to qualify for the 5 Percent Club. I think you have them in check. If you don't yet, call your advisor and make it so!

1. *Once you retire, keep $30,000 in a savings account.* That's your rainy day money for emergencies. Tuck it away. Forget about it.

2. *Invest the rest of your savings in a diversified portfolio of stocks and bonds.* With at least half of the money in stocks.

3. *Work out your living expenses and know what you need each month.* See how much is covered by Social Security, and other income sources.

4. *Start withdrawing five percent of your portfolio balance each year.* On Day One of your retirement, in twelve installments a year.

5. SPEND THE MONEY!
   I just wanted to make it abundantly clear, that you are approved to spend your withdrawal money. I repeat, you are **GO for spend**!

So, those are the five steps. Pretty straightforward once you make your mind up. A couple days organizing your expenses, talking to your advisor (or yourself, if you are your own advisor), and then setting up your accounts. You're done. You're set for retirement awesomeness.

The 5 Percent Club Rules.

OK, there *are* some rules to follow. We do have standards here in the 5 Percent Club that I am sure you will appreciate. Who am I kidding—these rules are simple and common-sense. Really, they have to do with **cutting out the noise—online, on TV, on the radio**.

Rule #1: Remove any stock tracking apps you may have from your phone.

If you are out at dinner, you don't need to know about the stock market. In fact, most of the time, you don't need to know every move the stock market makes. It goes up, it goes down. The market can be quick to spook, and reacts quickly to uncertainty, and the news is full of uncertainty. But reason nearly always wins.

So, review your quarterly statements to keep informed as to how the market shakes out every few months. And even then, think about your portfolio in the context of YEARS, not quarters. If you have a question at quarter-end, ask your advisor. Keep him or her on their toes!

Rule #2: Switch off the 24/7 financial news stations.

All of them. You can still get your news at 6 p.m. everyday. But please, banish the perpetual noise, veiled as objective discussion, from entering your home, and brain. You will remain more than adequately informed if you choose your once-a-day news source. You don't need to be plugged into the news cycle all day. Anyway, you're too busy living an awesome retirement, right?!

Rule #3: Ignore scary headlines on the internet about the economy or the stock market

And **unfollow** *any account on social media that uses scare tactics to reel you in.*

If it's fear-inducing, it's probably making you feel that way by design. As we said before, scary headlines get you to click on a webpage, which is the whole point; the web page rises up the Google ranks with each click, and that is the website owner's goal. If they use fearsome lies to hook you in, they almost certainly don't deserve your click. So please, don't reward fear-based marketing by clicking on those headlines. Shrug them off, and laugh them off, and know that you are not missing a single beat by not clicking on a scary headline.

Rule #4: Stay the course and keep informed.

Follow more academic, non-biased sources of information to keep informed as to your retirement choices. I share weekly articles, and have a radio show, and from time to time share some videos about topics *I* think are of interest, and I welcome you to check in. Find your objective voices of reason, and listen to them now and then, but mostly, live your life!

Rule #5: Live your life with a new sense of opportunity and creativity.

If there is a goal of the chapters in Part Three, it is that you connect to the idea that your retirement possibilities are truly brilliant. Each of us has a different talent, passion, or thing that drives us. I know that there are many retirees living truly awesome retirements; I learn from them every day. Some are clients, some are famous octogenarians, some I read about. The converse is also true. I see people in my office each day whose light is going out because they don't believe they deserve to have a good retirement. Whatever that voice is—whether it is deep-seated fear about moneyor just a resolute belief that spending is for fools—it needs a good talking-to because it's robbing some people of an inspired, fulfilling life … at a time when there should   be zero rules about living to the max, and YOU HAVE THE MONEY TO BE FREE!

At the end of the day, you can find a counter opinion to my opinion, and then another tangential counter opinion to that opinion. There are opinions everywhere you go in the media. Some people shout louder, and they get heard the most. There are those with compelling voices that win out over the reasoned voices. There are voices that use tactics to win your mind.

There are so many opinions out there and so much noise. About 95 percent of the opinions you hear about how you should approach your money are irrelevant to you, or can be harmful. Focus on the information that can make a real difference to your life. You know what you need to know, and when you are not sure, your judgment will usually keep you on track. Hopefully, the rules I left you with above will be of service as you navigate the information and guidance you want.

And What If I don't Have $200K in the Bank?

The reality is that you need $200,000 invested in at least 50 percent stocks, with a smart asset allocation plan, in order to be able to spend according to my plan. I hate to put an entry limit on the 5 Percent Club. But the reality is that the other half of America's retirees—who also of course number 23 million—do not have the same level of opportunity when it comes to spending their savings.

Of course, if you don't have $200,000 saved and you are about to retire, you can absolutely revolutionize your retirement. You have abundant choices with regard to how you live your retirement. Your financial plan should not be along the five percent spend-your-savings approach, and   I urge you to get independent financial advice. However, the mentality to live retirement according to your rules and dreams—that's the same for everyone embarking on retirement. And you still probably have more to spend than you think.

And if you still have some solid savings, then you still have good options. I'm happy that your generation has a solvent Social Security, and that you have employer retirement plans—much more so than the generations behind you.

Regardless of how much money you have saved for retirement, there are truths about the 5 Percent Club that apply to us all:

1. We will not be scared by daily shifts in the market, nor the media's response to downturns or random down days.
2. We keep our "nut" invested, because in 85 years, there has not been a 20- year period when the market has returned less than 8 percent.
3. It's your time IN the market, not TIMING the market.
4. YOUR Social Security is solvent. You are getting paid.
5. Keep your rainy day savings stashed away, and spend according to your budget—it's likely more than you think!
6. Live with OPTIMISM and a sense of POSSIBILITY!

The 5 Percent Club Pledge

So, I leave you with this pledge, which is really a pledge to yourself, and to your spouse if you're married. This pledge serves as an affirmation. If you are resolute in living your ultimate retirement and using the money you have saved to really go for what brings you contentment and fulfilment, this pledge is for you:

I declare that I am in charge of this exciting new chapter of my life. I have my budget in place, my investments thoughtfully allocated in a diversified portfolio of stocks and bonds with at least half of the money in stocks, and I spend five percent of my portfolio savings total each year.

I use this money to fulfill my dreams, to support people or causes I care about, with intention. I might change what I spend my money on, but each spending decision will be with the goal of LIVING MY MOST AWESOME RETIREMENT.

I am open to new experiences even if they're out of my personal comfort zone. I am ready to put my money to work as I see fit.

I'm aligned with my spouse and we made our plans together.

Do you have your own take on the 5 Percent Club pledge? I would love to hear it. I would love to hear your stories of how you put your retirement savings to work, to see them in action from day one of Retirement. Share your experiences with me on social media, and spread the word that there is another, more empowered, way to view retirement.

Be blessed,
Dave

Appendix:

The Rolling Periods Report
S&P 500 With Monthly Dividends

Appendix Explanation

The following illustration, if you understand it, could radically change the way you view investing in the stock market. The historical data below simply shows you what would have happened if you had retired in any given year (starting in 1931). Each "retirement" is assumed to last 20 Years.

The first row reveals what would have happened if someone retired in 1931 with $100,000. The money is invested in the 500 largest companies in the U.S. (otherwise known as the S&P 500 Index).

Starting with $100,000, the chart shows what would have happened if you starting withdrawing $5,000 per year beginning the very first year of retirement. In each example, over 20 years, you would have withdrawn a total of $100,000 ($5000 per year for 20 years).

So, if you retired in 1931, over the next 20 years your money would have grown to $513,210-even though you withdrew 5% of the original investment each year.

Important Points

1. 100% of the scenarios result in you ending up with more money than you started with.

2. The WORST period illustrated is from 1997-2017. Your original $100,000 would have ended with a value of $145,177 (even though you had been withdrawing $5000 per year for 20 years).

3. The BEST period illustrated is from 1979-1999. Your original $100,000 would have ended with a value of $1,840,805 (even though you had been withdrawing $5000 per year for 20 years).

4. The MEDIA period   illustrated is from 1953-1973 where your original investment would have grown to $552,969.

5. This is absolutely amazing news.

6. It is statistically correct to say, "Over the past 86 years, if you started with $100,000 and withdrew $5000 per year for 20 years, every time you would have ended up with more than the original investment."

STARTING RETIREMENT DATE	END	ORIGINAL INVESTMENT	TOTAL WITHDRAWAL (5% PER YEAR)	ANNUAL RETURN	ENDING VALUE
12/31/1931	12/31/1951	$100,000	$100,000	11.40%	$513,210
12/31/1932	12/31/1952	$100,000	$100,000	13.27%	$766,022
12/31/1933	12/31/1953	$100,000	$100,000	10.15%	$386,712
12/31/1934	12/31/1954	$100,000	$100,000	12.56%	$660,031
12/31/1935	12/31/1955	$100,000	$100,000	10.63%	$431,282
12/31/1936	12/31/1956	$100,000	$100,000	7.84%	$219,962
12/31/1937	12/31/1957	$100,000	$100,000	12.37%	$633,616
12/31/1938	12/31/1958	$100,000	$100,000	12.03%	$589,235
12/31/1939	12/31/1959	$100,000	$100,000	13.08%	$735,558
12/31/1940	12/31/1960	$100,000	$100,000	14.40%	$966,123
12/31/1941	12/31/1961	$100,000	$100,000	16.91%	$1,585,122
12/31/1942	12/31/1962	$100,000	$100,000	15.46%	$1,194,776
12/31/1943	12/31/1963	$100,000	$100,000	15.13%	$1,118,421
12/31/1944	12/31/1964	$100,000	$100,000	14.89%	$1,066,591
12/31/1945	12/31/1965	$100,000	$100,000	13.39%	$786,149
12/31/1946	12/31/1966	$100,000	$100,000	13.87%	$867,869
12/31/1947	12/31/1967	$100,000	$100,000	14.87%	$1,062,546
12/31/1948	12/31/1968	$100,000	$100,000	15.35%	$1,169,095
12/31/1949	12/31/1969	$100,000	$100,000	14.07%	$903,770
12/31/1950	12/31/1970	$100,000	$100,000	12.70%	$679,685
12/31/1951	12/31/1971	$100,000	$100,000	12.15%	$604,166
12/31/1952	12/31/1972	$100,000	$100,000	12.10%	$597,148
12/31/1953	12/31/1973	$100,000	$100,000	11.74%	$552,969
12/31/1954	12/31/1974	$100,000	$100,000	7.97%	$227,119
12/31/1955	12/31/1975	$100,000	$100,000	7.57%	$204,629
12/31/1956	12/31/1976	$100,000	$100,000	8.21%	$241,785
12/31/1957	12/31/1977	$100,000	$100,000	8.98%	$292,907
12/31/1958	12/31/1978	$100,000	$100,000	6.99%	$174,859
12/31/1959	12/31/1979	$100,000	$100,000	7.03%	$176,891
12/31/1960	12/31/1980	$100,000	$100,000	8.38%	$252,335
12/31/1961	12/31/1981	$100,000	$100,000	6.57%	$155,386
12/31/1962	12/31/1982	$100,000	$100,000	8.37%	$251,568
12/31/1963	12/31/1983	$100,000	$100,000	7.80%	$217,461

12/31/1964	12/31/1984	$100,000	$100,000	7.00%	$175,399
12/31/1965	12/31/1985	$100,000	$100,000	7.25%	$187,660
12/31/1966	12/31/1986	$100,000	$100,000	9.36%	$321,308
12/31/1967	12/31/1987	$100,000	$100,000	7.91%	$223,717
12/31/1968	12/31/1988	$100,000	$100,000	7.85%	$220,163
12/31/1969	12/31/1989	$100,000	$100,000	10.32%	$402,199
12/31/1970	12/31/1990	$100,000	$100,000	10.28%	$398,713
12/31/1971	12/31/1991	$100,000	$100,000	10.60%	$428,851
12/31/1972	12/31/1992	$100,000	$100,000	9.60%	$340,207
12/31/1973	12/31/1993	$100,000	$100,000	11.98%	$583,058
12/31/1974	12/31/1994	$100,000	$100,000	14.84%	$1,055,377
12/31/1975	12/31/1995	$100,000	$100,000	14.36%	$958,459
12/31/1976	12/31/1996	$100,000	$100,000	14.00%	$891,251
12/31/1977	12/31/1997	$100,000	$100,000	16.44%	$1,447,113
12/31/1978	12/31/1998	$100,000	$100,000	17.64%	$1,818,318
12/31/1979	12/31/1999	$100,000	$100,000	17.70%	$1,840,805
12/31/1980	12/31/2000	$100,000	$100,000	15.40%	$1,180,094
12/31/1981	12/31/2001	$100,000	$100,000	15.50%	$1,202,665
12/31/1982	12/31/2002	$100,000	$100,000	13.25%	$763,294
12/31/1983	12/31/2003	$100,000	$100,000	13.34%	$777,933
12/31/1984	12/31/2004	$100,000	$100,000	13.75%	$845,961
12/31/1985	12/31/2005	$100,000	$100,000	12.38%	$634,571
12/31/1986	12/31/2006	$100,000	$100,000	12.15%	$603,834
12/31/1987	12/31/2007	$100,000	$100,000	12.30%	$624,349
12/31/1988	12/31/2008	$100,000	$100,000	9.51%	$332,734
12/31/1989	12/31/2009	$100,000	$100,000	8.92%	$288,562
12/31/1990	12/31/2010	$100,000	$100,000	10.00%	$373,397
12/31/1991	12/31/2011	$100,000	$100,000	8.57%	$264,524
12/31/1992	12/31/2012	$100,000	$100,000	8.95%	$290,416
12/31/1993	12/31/2013	$100,000	$100,000	9.73%	$350,521
12/31/1994	12/31/2014	$100,000	$100,000	10.48%	$417,526
12/31/1995	12/31/2015	$100,000	$100,000	8.58%	$265,008
12/31/1996	12/31/2016	$100,000	$100,000	7.76%	$214,933
12/31/1997	12/31/2017	$100,000	$100,000	6.33%	$145,177

Investments are not FDIC - insured, nor are they deposits of or guaranteed by a bank or any other entity, so they may lose value.

Figures shown are past results and are not predictive of results in future periods. Current and future results may be lower or higher than those shown. Share prices and returns will vary, so investors may lose money. Investing for short periods makes losses more likely.

Regular investing does not ensure a profit or protect against loss. Investors should consider their willingness to keep investing when share prices are declining. Market indexes are unmanaged and, therefore, have no expenses. Investors cannot invest directly in an index. Results for the Lipper indexes do not reflect sales charges. There have been periods when the fund has lagged the index.

The illustration included herein does not reflect the effects of taxes in some or all of the investments. The Rolling Periods Report shows the selected security's total return performance over different periods of a specified length. For example, a report might show all of the three year rolling periods between 1980 and 1995. The report indicates in its sub-heading the length of the periods and the time frame it covers. Information on the initial investment, sales charge, reinvestment of dividends, and reinvestment of capital is displayed above the column headings. These figures reflect historical data and are not indicators of the security's future performance.

Keep in mind that indices are unmanaged and their results do not reflect sales charges, commissions or expenses. Additionally, they should only be used for general comparisons over meaningful time frames. S&P 500 with Monthly Dividends is an unmanaged market capitalization weighted price index composed of 500 widely held common stocks listed on the New York Stock Exchange, American Stock Exchange and Over-The-Counter market. The value of the index varies with the aggregate value of the common equity of each of the 500 companies. The stocks represented by this index involve investment risks which may include the loss of principal invested.

Data and calculations provided by Thompson-Reuters

Notes:

Part One

Chapter One

[1] (i.) Deloitte University Press. (2015). The Future of Wealth in the United States. https://www2.deloitte.com/content/dam/insights/us/articles/us-generational- wealth-trends/DUP_1371_Future-wealth-in-America_MASTER.pdf

(ii.) Oxford Economics. (2016, September). The Longevity Economy. https://www.aarp.org/content/dam/aarp/research/surveys_statistics/econ/2017/201 6-natl-longevity-economy.doi.10.26419%252Fres.00172.001.pdf

(iii.) Investopedia. (2018) https://www.investopedia.com/terms/b/baby_boomer.asp

[2] Insured Retirement Institute. (2017). Boomer Expectations for Retirement. https://www.myirionline.org/docs/default-source/research/iri_boomers- expectations-for-retirement-2017.pdf

[3] Biggs, A. (2016, July 16). Why Retirees Aren't Running Out of Money. *Forbes.* https://www.forbes.com/sites/andrewbiggs/2016/07/14/retirees-arent-running- out-of-money-but-why/#1996b6e83853

[4] Browning, C., Guo, T., Cheng, Y. and Finke, M. (2016). "Spending in Retirement: Determining the Consumption Gap." *Journal of Financial Planning* 29 (2): 42–53.

[5] Health and Retirement Study. (2017, January). Produced and distributed by the University of Michigan with funding from the National Institute on Aging (grant number NIA U01AG009740). http://hrsonline.isr.umich.edu/sitedocs/databook/?page=1

Chapter Two

[6] Oakley, D. & Kenneally, K. (2017, February). Retirement Security 2017: A Roadmap for Policy Makers Americans' Views of the Retirement

Crisis and Solutions. *National Institute on Retirement Security.* https://www. nirsonline.org/reports/retirement-security-2017-americans-views-of- the-retirement-crisis/

[7] Biggs, A. (2015, July 9). Good News: Retirement Income Still Being Undercounted. *Forbes.* https://www.forbes.com/sites/ andrewbiggs/2015/07/09/good-news-retirement- income-still-being-undercounted/#2d9feab2397f

[8] Poterba, J., Venti, S., and Wise, D. (2013). "Correction: The Composition and Drawdown of Wealth in Retirement." *Journal of Economic Perspectives*, 27 (4): 219-22.

[9] The PEW Charitable Trust (2016, September 14). Employer-Sponsored Retirement Plan Access, Uptake and Savings. http://www.pewtrusts.org/en/ research-and-analysis/issue- briefs/2016/09/employer-sponsored-retirement-plan-access-uptake-and-savings

[10] Foster, A. (2016, September 16). A Closer Look at Spending Patterns in Older Americans. *Bureau of Labor Statistics.* https://www.bls.gov/opub/btn/ volume- 5/mobile/spending-patterns-of-older-americans.htm

[11] Insured Retirement Institute. (2017). Baby Boomer Expectations for Retirement 2017. http://www.irionline.org/resources/resources-detail-view/iri-baby-boomer- expectations-for-retirement-2017

[12] National Institute on Retirement Security. (2016, March 1). Shortchanged in Retirement: Continuing Challenges to Women's Financial Future. https://www.nirsonline.org/wp- content/uploads/2016/03/2016_ shortchanged_powerpoint.pdf

[13] Rolling Periods Report. See Appendix.

[14] Biggs, A. (2016, July 16). Why Retirees Aren't Running Out of Money. *Forbes.* https://www.forbes.com/sites/andrewbiggs/2016/07/14/retirees-arent-running- out-of-money-but-why/#1996b6e83853

[15] Derousseau, R. (2017, October 25). Retiring Soon? You May Spend a Lot Less Than You Expect. *Fortune Magazine.* http://fortune. com/2017/10/25/retirement-costs- lower/

[16] Money-Zine. (2017, October 26). Retiring with a Mortgage. https:// www.money-zine.com/financial-planning/retirement/retiring-with-a-mortgage/

Chapter Three

[17] Bureau of Labor Statistics. (2002, March 2). Consumer Price Index for the Elderly. https://www.bls.gov/opub/ted/2012/ted_20120302.htm

[18] American Hospital Association. How Boomers Will Change Healthcare. https://www.aha.org/system/files/content/00-10/070508-boomerreport.pdf

[19] Medicare.gov information: https://www.medicare.gov/pubs/pdf/10050-Medicare-and-You.pdf

[20] Benz, C. (2017, August 31). 75 Must-Know Statistics About Long-Term Care. *Morningstar.* http://www.morningstar.com/articles/823957/75-mustknow-statistics- about-longterm-care.html

[21] Costs of Care. Updated (2017, October 10). *U.S. Department of Health and Human Services.* https://longtermcare.acl.gov/costs-how-to-pay/costs-of-care.html

[22] Medicare.gov: Your Medicare Coverage - Long-term Care. https://www.medicare.gov/coverage/long-term-care.html

[23] O'Connor, A. (2018, March 5). Millennials More Susceptible to Scams Than Seniors. *AARP.* https://www.aarp.org/money/scams-fraud/info-2018/millennial- scams-fd.html

[24] Consumer Sentinel Network Data Book 2017: Report Categories. *Federal Trade Commission.* Accessed March 2018. https://www.ftc.gov/policy/reports/policy- reports/commission-staff-reports/consumer-sentinel-network-data-book- 2017/report-categories

Chapter Four

[25] Levisohn, B. (2016, Feb 10). Be Afraid: Dow Drops 100 Points as Bears Maul Bulls. *Barron's.* https://www.barrons.com/articles/be-afraid-dow-drops-100- points-as-bears-maul-bulls-1455145027

[26] Lombardi, M. (2016, April 8). The Imminent 2016 Stock Market Crash. *Profit Confidential.* https://www.profitconfidential.com/stock-market/the-imminent-2016- stock-market-crash/

[27] Lewitinn, L. (2016, March 10). We Have Just Witnessed a 'Death Cross' in the Market's Fear Indicator. *Yahoo.com* https://finance.yahoo.com/news/we-have-just- witnessed-a--death-cross--in-the-market-s-fear-indicator-200044838.html

[28] Zeiler, D. (2016, March 9). This Will Make the Next Stock Market Crash as Bad as 2008. *WallStreetExaminer.com* http://wallstreetexaminer.com/2016/03/will-make- next-stock-market-crash-bad-2008/#

[29] Laughlin, L. (2016, March 29). "Here's Another Sign a Recession is Coming."*Fortune.com.* http://fortune.com/2016/03/29/recession-corporate-profits/

[30] Sageworks Stats. (2013, May 26). 4 Things You Don't Know About Private Companies. *Forbes.* https://www.forbes.com/sites/sageworks/2013/05/26/4-things- you-dont-know-about-private-companies/#6b0eccc6291a

[31] Damodaran, A. (2018, January 5). Annual Returns on Stock, T.Bonds and T.Bills: 1928 - Current. *NYU Stern School of Business.* http://pages.stern.nyu.edu/~adamodar/New_Home_Page/datafile/histretSP.html

[32] Economic Policy Institute. (2017, May 30). Here is What's at Stake with the Conflict of Interest ('Fiduciary') Rule. https://www.epi.org/publication/here-is- whats-at-stake-with-the-conflict-of-interest-fiduciary-rule/

Part Two

Chapter Seven

[33] Damodaran, A. (2018, January 5). Annual Returns on Stock, T.Bonds and T.Bills: 1928 - Current. *NYU Stern School of Business.* http://pages.stern.nyu.edu/~adamodar/New_Home_Page/datafile/histretSP.

[34] Bernstein, W. (2002). Only Two Centuries of Data. *Efficient Frontier.* http://www.efficientfrontier.com/ef/402/2cent.htm

[35] Global Wealth Report. (2017, January). *Credit Suisse* - Research Institute. http://publications.credit-suisse.com/tasks/render/file/index.cfm?fileid=12DFFD63- 07D1-EC63-A3D5F67356880EF3

Chapter Ten

[36] Gallup. (2016, May). Majority in US do not have a Will. http://news.gallup.com/poll/191651/majority-not.aspx

[37] Frequently Asked Questions on Gift Taxes (2017, Oct 23). IRS.gov https://www.irs.gov/businesses/small-businesses-self-employed/frequently-asked- questions-on-gift-taxes

Part Three

Chapter Eleven

[38] Carter, J. (1998). Virtues of Aging. *Ballantine Books.*

[39] Schlossberg, N. (2003) Retire Smart, Retire Happy. *American Psychological Association* (APA).

[40] Moon JR., Glymour MM,. Subramanian SV,. Avendaño M, Kawachi I. (2012, August). Transition to retirement and risk of cardiovascular disease: prospective analysis of the US health and retirement study. *Social Science & Medicine.* 75(3):526- 30.

[41] Kesavayuth, Dusanee & Rosenman, Robert & Zikos, Vasileios. (2016). The dynamic effects of retirement on well-being. 10.13140/RG.2.2.23007.25764.

[42] Desilver, D. (2016, June 20). More older Americans are working, and working more, than they used to. *Pew Research Center.* http://www.pewresearch.org/fact-tank/2016/06/20/more-older-americans-are-working-and-working-more-than- they-used-to/

[43] Wang, Mo & Shi, Junqi. (2013). Psychological Research on Retirement. Annual review of psychology. 65. 10.1146/annurev-psych-010213-115131.

[44] Yujie Zhan, MS, Mo Wang, PhD, and Songqi Liu, MS, University of Maryland; Kenneth S. Shultz, PhD, California State University, San Bernardino. (2009). "Bridge Employment and Retirees' Health: A Longitudinal Investigation," *Journal of Occupational Health Psychology*, Vol. 14, No. 4.

[45] Corporate for National and Community Service. (2007). A Research Brief on Volunteer Retention and Turnover. https://www.nationalservice.gov/pdf/07_0307_boomer_report.pdf

Chapter Thirteen

[46] Gottman, J. & Silver, N. (2015). Seven Principles for Making Marriage Work. *Random House/Crown/Harmony.*

[47] Bach, D. (2004) Smart Couples Finish Rich: 9 Steps to Creating a Rich Future for You and Your Partner. *New York: Broadway Books.*

[48] Burns Kingbury, K. (2017). Breaking Money Silence®: How to Shatter Money Taboos, Talk More Openly about Finances, and Live a Richer Life. *Praeger.*

[49] Volpe-Kohler, M. (2017, December). The Financial Literacy Gender Gap is Narrowing—Here's How You Can Help Close It. *FINRA.* http://www.finra.org/investors/highlights/financial-literacy-gender-gap-how-you-can-help-close-it

[50] MoneyTips. (2016, June 2). Men Vs. Women: Who Makes The Financial Decisions? *Huffington Post.* https://www.huffingtonpost.com/moneytips/men-vs-women-who-makes-th_b_10237306.html

[51] Hopkins, J. & Littell, D. (2017). 2017 RICP ® Retirement Income Literacy Gender Differences Report. *American College of Financial Services.* http://retirement.theamericancollege.edu/sites/retirement/files/Gender_Differences_in_Retirement_Income_Literacy_Report.pdf

Made in the USA
Columbia, SC
05 December 2020